Authors typically dedicate their books to people they know – a beloved teacher, their children, or perhaps their parents. In this case, I want to reach out to an entirely different audience.

I dedicate this to those who disagree with me and whose lives run contrary to my conclusions. It's only by reaching out to those who we disagree with that we can ever hope to move forward, isn't it?

Islam's Apology

Islam's Apology

A People's Crime

Jean-Paul Prophète

Paltz Press

Sale of this book without a front cover may be unauthorized. If this book is coverless, it may have been reported to the publisher as "unsold or destroyed" and neither the author nor the publisher may have received payment for it.

Copyright © 2013 by J.P. Prophète

All rights reserved. No part of this book may be reproduced in any form without written permission except in the case of brief quotations embodied in critical articles and reviews. For information, please contact the publisher.

This is a work of fiction. Names, characters, places and incidents either are products of the author's imagination or are used fictitiously. Any resemblance to actual events or locales or persons, living or dead, is entirely coincidental.

First Printing, 2017

Printed in the United States of America

ISBN: 978-0-692-99920-2

Paltz Press, NY
Contact@PaltzPress.com

Contents

List of Maps   9

Timeline   13

Glossary   15

Preface   21

Part One – Muntik Arrives   27
1. The Return of Muntik   28
2. Muntik's Message   32

Part Two – Muntik versus the Motheyeen   35
1. Taqiyya and its Limits   36
2. The Islamic View of Women   40
3. When did the Prophet Muhammad Marry Aisha?   58
4. Muslims and the Prevalence of Terrorism   65
5. Islam's Commandment of Killing Non-Muslims   68
6. The Practice of Stoning in Islam   77
7. Virgins in Heaven   82
8. Islam on Slavery and its Reformation   86
9. Silence   94

Part Three – The Fall   95
1. Is Celebrating Christmas Permissible?   96
2. Is Listening to Songs and Music Permissible?   100
3. Are Tattoos Permissible?   107
4. Is Growing a Beard Obligatory?   110
5. Is the Hijab Obligatory?   114
6. What are the Boundaries of Gender in Marriage?   120
7. Were the Prophets Infallible?   124
8. Defeat   132

Part Four – A New Embrace   133
1. Who (what) is Allah?   134
2. What is a Muslim?   135

3.	Islamic God vs Judeo-Christian God	136
4.	The Islamic View on Jesus	137
5.	The Islamic View on the Original Sin	141
6.	The Crescent Moon	143
7.	What is Ramadan?	144
8.	The Sacredness of Churches	146
9.	The Fate of non-Muslims	148
10.	The Religions of the Prophets	151
11.	Becoming the Perfect Muslim	153
12.	Sunnis and Shias	155

Part Five – Farewell 158
   1. Muntik's Departure 159

Footnotes Appendices 164

Endnotes 166

Maps

600 AD – 750 CE……………………………………………..p. 10

969 AD – 1258 CE……………...…………………………p. 11

1517 AD – 1900 CE…………...…………………………...p. 12

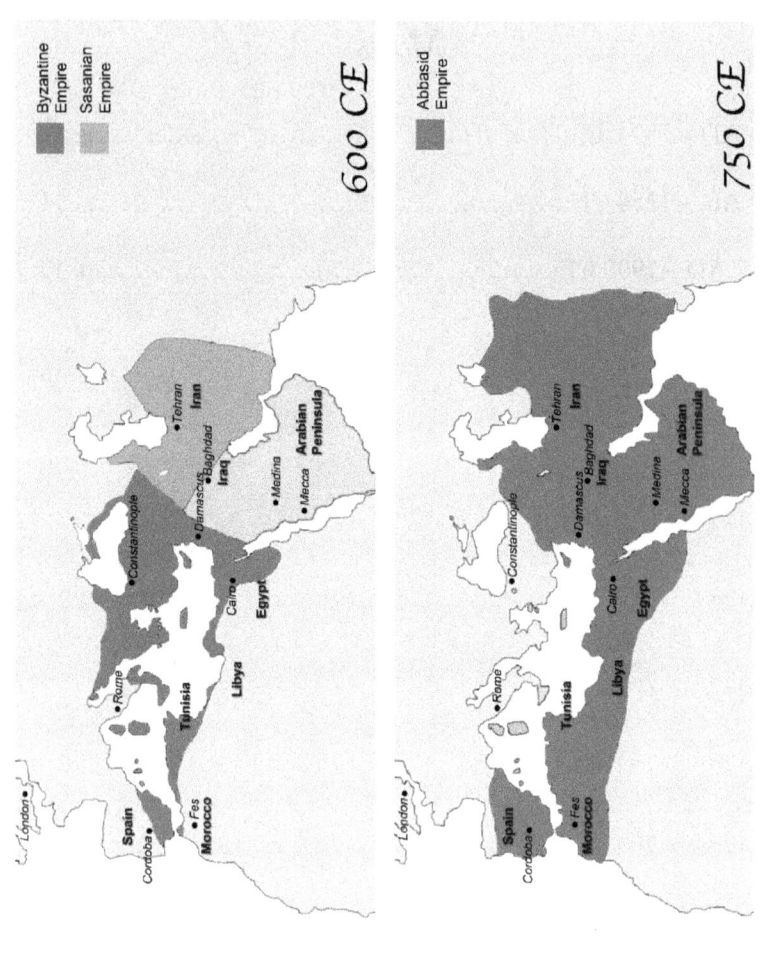

600 – 750 CE

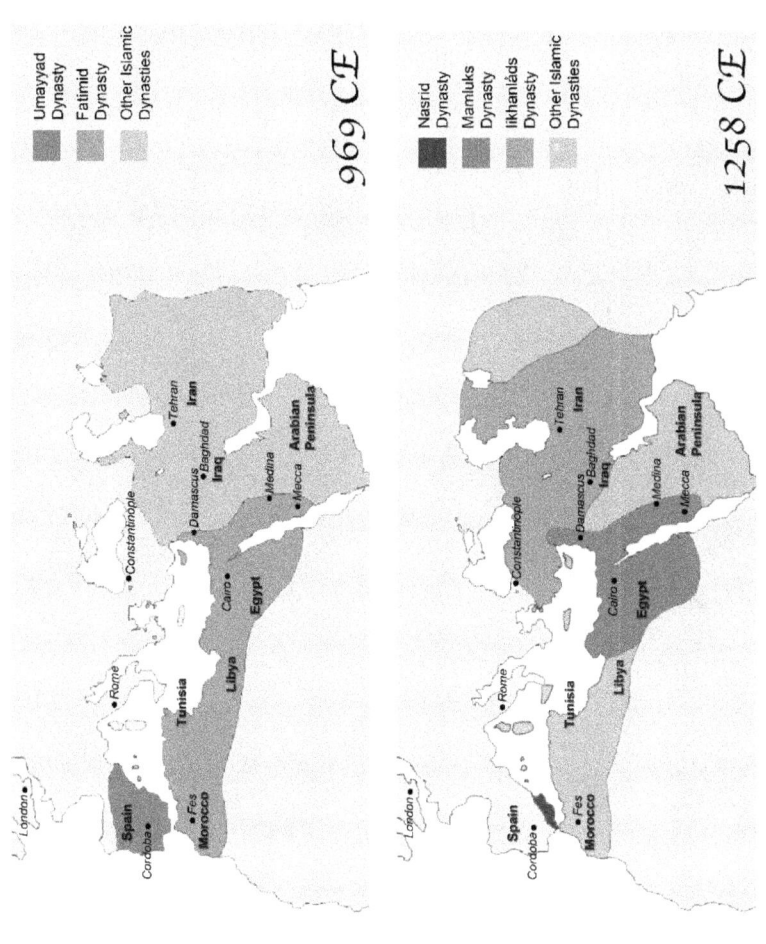

969 – 1258 CE

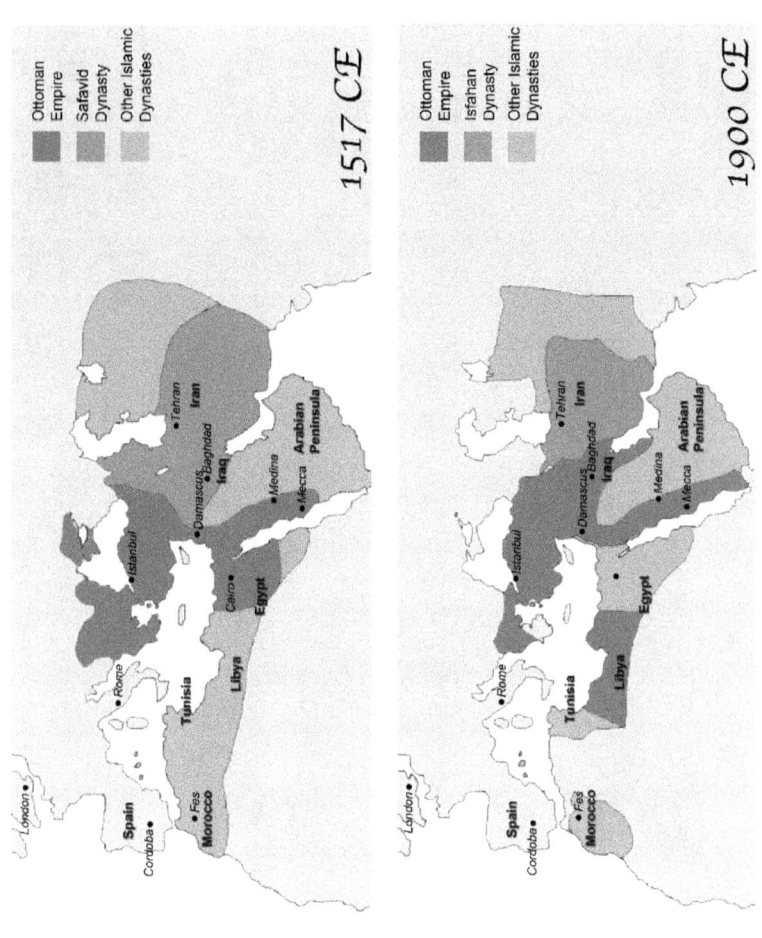

1517 – 1900 CE

Timeline

~3100 BCE	The first Egyptian dynasty is established
~1010 BCE	The Prophet David becomes the king of Israel
~959 BCE	The Prophet Solomon builds the first Jewish temple in the city of Jerusalem
~469 BCE	Socrates is born
~4 BCE	Jesus is born
~30	The Romans crucify Jesus
79	Mount Vesuvius erupts destroying the towns of Pompeii and Herculaneum
~380	Christianity becomes the official religion of the Roman Empire
~400	St. Augustine writes *The Confessions*
512	The first inscription in Arabic is recorded
570	The Prophet Muhammad is born
610	The Prophet Muhammad receives his first revelation
615	The Prophet Muhammad and his companions escape persecution in Mecca and flee to Abyssinia (modern-day Ethiopia)
622	The Prophet Muhammad and his companions migrate to Yathrib (modern-day Medina); this is known as the great hijrah
630	The Prophet Muhammad capitulates the city of Mecca
632	The Prophet Muhammad dies and Abu Bakr becomes the first caliph of Islam
656	Imam Ali becomes the fourth caliph of Islam following Uthman's assassination
661	Imam Ali is assassinated. Muawiyah founds the Umayyad dynasty in Damascus
691	Caliph Abdel-Malik completes the Dome of the Rock
750	Abu al-Abbas as-Saffah overthrows the Umayyad dynasty and becomes the first caliph of the Abbasid dynasty
762	The Abbasid dynasty moves the caliphate to Baghdad
800	Pope Leo III crowns Charlemagne as "Emperor of the Romans"

969	The Fatimids conquer Egypt and move their capital to Cairo
1040	The Seljuk Turks conquer territories in Persia
1095	Pope Urban II delivers his speech at the Council of Clermont inspiring the First Crusade War
1299	The Ottoman Empire is founded
1347	The Bubonic Plague spreads across Europe
1448	Johannes Gutenberg invents the printing press
1478	The Spanish Inquisition is established
1498	Leonardo da Vinci completes *The Last Supper*
1501	The Safavid dynasty was founded in Iran
1509	Henry VIII becomes the king of England
1517	Martin Luther posts his 95 *Theses* on the door of the All Saints' Church in Wittenberg, Germany
1618	The Thirty Years War begins
1651	English Civil War between the Parliamentarians and the Royalists ends
1692	The Salem Witch Trials of Massachusetts begins
1666	The Great Fire of London devastates the majority of central London
1715	King Louis XIV of France dies
1776	Adam Smith publishes *The Wealth of Nations*
1833	The UK parliament passes the Slavery Abolition Act
1865	Abraham Lincoln is assassinated
1917	The Balfour Declaration is created
1918	World War I ends
1945	World War II ends
1948	The first Arab-Israeli war begins
1956	Gamal Abdel-Nasser becomes the president of Egypt
1979	Saddam Hussein becomes the president of Iraq
1988	The Iran-Iraq War ends
2001	Al-Qaeda terrorists fly airplanes into the World Trade Center
2003	The United States invades Iraq
2011	Osama bin Laden is killed

Glossary

Below is a translation of Arabic words and Islamic historical figures used in this book to help guide readers.

Abeed: Slaves, servants, or those who are totally subordinated; singular, abd

Abeed'allah: Servants of God; singular, abd'allah or abdullah

Abu Bakr: The father-in-law and one of the earliest companions of the Prophet Muhammad. Abu Bakr served as the first caliph following the Prophet Muhammad's death

Ahadith: Recorded sayings of the Prophet Muhammad. They are used alongside the Quran as a tool towards assessing matters of Islamic jurisprudence; singular, hadith

Aisha: A wife of the Prophet Muhammad and daughter of Abu Bakr

Al-Fatiha: Literally translates into "the opening." It is the first chapter of the Quran

Al-Masjid al-Haram: Also known as the Grand Mosque, it is the mosque in Mecca that surrounds the Ka'aba

Allah: God

Asma: The elder sister of Aisha and daughter of Abu Bakr

Battle of Badr: The first major battle between the Prophet Muhammad and the pagans of Pre-Islamic Arabia. The Prophet Muhammad and his companions were victorious

Battle of Uhud: The second major battle between the Prophet Muhammad and the Pagans of Pre-Islamic Arabia. The Prophet Muhammad and his companions were defeated

Bilal: A slave who was emancipated by Abu Bakr. A companion of the Prophet Muhammad, Bilal is mostly recognized for his role in making the calls for prayer

Burqa: Clothing that covers the entire body and face, including the eyes

Caliph: Successor. This role was given to the individual who would serve as both the political and religious figurehead of the ummah

Cave of Hira: Located in Mecca, it is believed that the Prophet Muhammad first received God's revelations while inside this cave

Daff: Tambourine

Eid: Festival or holiday

Fatimah: A daughter of the Prophet Muhammad and the wife of Imam Ali.

Hajj: Holy pilgrimage. As one of the pillars of Islam, all able-bodied Muslims are required to take part in the hajj, which occurs during the twelfth month of the Islamic lunar calendar, at least once in their lives

Halal: That which is permissible

Hanafi: One of the four major schools of thought on Sunnis Islamic law

Haram: That which is forbidden or prohibited

Harb: War

Hijab: Quranically, hijab refers to a barrier between two objects. In the vernacular, the hijab is an article of clothing that covers the head and neck of an individual

Hijrah: Migration. Historically, the hijrah refers to the great migration that the Prophet Muhammad and his companions made from Mecca to Medina in 622 CE. This journey marked the date of the beginning of the Islamic lunar calendar

Houris: Beings (traditionally regarded as women) of perfect beauty in paradise

Imam: In Sunnism, imams typically refer to individuals who lead prayers. While the same meaning is found in Shiism, the word imam also denotes those individuals who are leaders of an Islamic community and provide guidance; in mainstream Shiism, there are 12 central imams

Imam al-Shafi'i: Born in 767 CE, he is regarded by many Muslims as one of the greatest legal theorists in Islamic history

Imam Ali: The cousin and son-in-law of the Prophet Muhammad. He was the son of Abu Talib, the Prophet Muhammad's uncle. He was the first male, after the Prophet Muhammad, to embrace Islam. Imam Ali served as the fourth caliph following the Prophet Muhammad's death, and is a central figure in Shia Islam

Imam Mahdi: According to Shia Islam, Imam Mahdi is the last of the twelve imams. He is believed to be in occultation and will return with the Jesus to restore peace to the world. In Sunnis Islam, the Mahdi has not yet been born and therefore his identity is unknown.

Islam: Submission

Jihad: Struggling, or striving

Ka'aba: A cube-shaped structure located in the Masjid al-Haram mosque, of which is within the city of Mecca. It is believed to be built by the Prophet Adam and then reconstructed by the Prophet Abraham. The Ka'aba is regarded as the first "House of God" on Earth where humans could worship God.

Kazab: One who lies

Khimar: Literally translates into "to cover." Often used to refer to a type of clothing that covers the head

Mecca: A city in Saudi Arabia and home to the Ka'aba. In Islamic history, Mecca is the birthplace of the Prophet Muhammad and was the place where the Quran was revealed. Mecca is generally regarded as the holiest city in Islam and is the site of the hajj

Mukham: With respect to the Quran, mukham refers to Quranic verses whose meaning is clear and easily understood

Muntik: Logic

Mutashabih: With respect to the Quran, mukham refers to Quranic verses whose meaning is not clear and requires deeper interpretation

Motheyeen: Mischief

Muqaddas: Holy

Muslim: One who submits

Niqab: Clothing that covers the face, but with an exposed slit for the eyes

Quran: Literally translates into "recitation." It is the sacred religious scripture of Islam

Quraysh: One of the most powerful tribes of Pre-Islamic Arabia. The Prophet Muhammad was born to the Banu Hashim clan of the Quraysh tribe. During the rise of Islam, the Quraysh were strictly opposed to the Prophet Muhammad and his teachings

Rajm: Stoning

Ramadan: The ninth month of the Islamic lunar calendar. This was the month when the Quran was revealed and when Muslims are required to fast from sunrise to sunset

Sakheef: Ridiculous

Shaitan: Devil

Shias: A term for the followers of Shiism, one of the two main branches of Islam; singular, Shia.

Sooilfahim: Misconception

Sunnah: In Islamic theology, sunnah refers to the practices of the Prophet Muhammad

Sunnis: A term for the followers of Sunnism, one of the two main branches of Islam; singular, Sunni

Surah: A chapter of the Quran

Taif: A city located in the southeastern province of Mecca

Taqiyya: Religious dissimulation; i.e. concealing one's faith in order to avoid physical or mental harm

Tarke Awla: Abandoning that which is better

Treaty of Hudaybiyyah: A ten-year peace deal signed on 628 CE between the Quraysh and the Prophet Muhammad.

Turbah: A clay tablet that touches the forehead during prostration. This is typically used by Shias during prayer.

Umar: The second caliph following the Prophet Muhammad's death.

Ummah: Community or nation. This word is particularly used to describe all Muslims as a collective people under a single [Islamic] community

Umrah: Like the hajj, the umrah is a pilgrimage but is of lesser religious significance. It is optional and can be performed at any point in time

Uthman: The third caliph following the Prophet Muhammad's death

Wudu: An ablution that is performed before prayer

Yathrib: Modern day Medina

Zakat: Alms-giving. As one of the five pillars of Islam, all able-bodied Muslims are required to donate 2.5% of their savings towards charity

Zina: Unlawful sexual intercourse, including both fornication and adultery

Preface

During my third year of college, my philosophy advisor recommended that I apply to an upcoming conference focusing on religion and philosophy. Eager to attend but unsure what to write about, I opted to go with the suggested theme of the conference: How can we form rational discussions into the legitimacy of religious traditions?

Uncertain of where to begin, I hoped my friends could help me with a starting point. Unfortunately, each and everyone one of them answered with the same two words: "It's impossible." Refusing to believe that rational dialogue on the subject of religious legitimacy was indeed futile, I ultimately formed what I thought was the only method of fostering such discussions. Drawing on the philosophies of Socrates, John Hick, and Jean-Paul Sartre, I stressed the importance of shedding preconceived notions, inquiring into religious beliefs (rather than blindly accepting them), emphasizing religious pluralism, and recognizing that each individual's actions directly impacts society. I concluded that the only way society can hope to form rational discussions on the legitimacy of religious traditions is through raising a generation that is open-minded and challenges inherited knowledge.

Hoping to make more of an impact on the possibility of fostering genuine and progressive dialogue on religions beliefs and traditions than by presenting a 6-page paper to a room of some 30 people in the outskirts of Pennsylvania, I began answering religious questions, particularly on Islam, on online forums. To my great disappointment, I noticed that a large number of threads lacked any serious analytical discourse. Relaying the opinion of a religious scholar without any details explaining the rationale behind their judgment satisfied most religious inquiries. To me, this method of understanding religion was unacceptable as it failed to utilize any objective or critical scrutiny. While it is true that religious authorities have dedicated their lives to religion and have extensively studied the scriptures, they still remain fallible. Many of us with religious queries often blindly accept whatever input a prominent religious figure provides; this has undoubtedly led us in a downward spiral.

How can we as theists openly discuss, let alone defend, our religious beliefs to the opposition if we are unable to explain our own position? At its very core, religious acceptance is based on faith. However, such loyal conviction is simply not enough to shield religion from public scrutiny. Religion will not survive unless it is able to convince its audience. Such conviction can only permeate through the utilization of rationale and logic. Plainly speaking, religion must make sense. So long as theists continue to neglect and toss aside reason, the impression of religious beliefs will inevitably change.

There are a gross amount of misconceptions that exist about every faith. Today, some religions face harsher scrutiny and suffer more from widespread misconceptions than others. In a post 9/11 era, much of the world's attention is now on Islam. It is difficult, if not impossible, to read the news and not see at least one story on Islam and Muslims, whether it is about the religious and political feuds in the Middle East or a terrorist attack in Pakistan or Iraq. Over the last few years, a number of stereotypes and generalizations about Islam and Muslims in the Western world have formed. Unfortunately, the West has allowed itself to generalize these stereotypes and perceive them as truths. Due to the misconceptions that Westerners have about Islam and the misunderstandings that many Muslims themselves have about the Islamic faith, a growing number of people possess a misinformed view of the true teachings of Islam.

During the 2012 presidential debates, Herman Cain[i] and Newt Gingrich[ii] repeatedly emphasized that not all Muslims are true American citizens and that unless a Muslim could prove his loyalty to the United States, they would not appoint one to office. These statements are similar in nature to those of Glenn Beck, who asserted that 10% of all Muslims are terrorists[iii]; this is slightly better than Brigitte Gabriel's estimate of 15-25%[iv]. With such rhetoric, it is hardly surprising to hear reports such as that of the Iraqi woman in California who was beaten to death; her assaulter left with a note saying: "Go back to your country."[v] And what of the incident of a man who shot pellet bullets at the head and neck of another man because he thought he was Middle Eastern or Muslim[vi], or of Joshua Scaggs, who yelled in a train station: "This is my country!" and then slashed the throat of a University of Illinois law professor thinking he was Middle Eastern[vii].

And what of the American founding principle of freedom of religion and its recent disregard for Islam? On August 25th in 2010, a mosque in California was vandalized with graffiti stating: "No temple for the God of terrorism at Ground Zero"[viii] with similar vandalism occurring at the Madera mosque in California a couple weeks later on September 7th[ix]. What about the growing number of arson attacks against mosques across the United States? Unfortunately, such reports have barely scratched the surface of the degree of Islamophobia that has taken hold of this nation. Who can forget the Texas Board of Education's approval of a resolution calling for a limit on the number of Islamic references in Texas textbooks[x], or the American Muslim who was denied a foster child because she doesn't eat pork[xi], or Governor Bobby Jindal's support of using state funds to send students to religiously-affiliated schools only to cause Louisiana representative Valarie Hodges to withdraw her support after realizing that this would include Islamic schools[xii], or Arizona Governor Jan Brewer astoundingly prejudice comment:

> If you know Middle Easterners, a lot of them, they look Mexican or they look, you know, like a lot of people in South America, dark skin, dark hair, brown eyes ... And those people, their only goal in life is to, to cause harm to the United States. So why do we want them here, either legally or illegally?[xiii]

A poll commissioned by the Arab American Institute found that 57% of Republicans had an unfavorable opinion on Muslims; when it came to American Muslims, the number dropped slightly to 47%.[xiv] With figures like these, there is no denying that there is a serious problem with America's perceptions on Islam and Muslims. It is time now more than ever to confront the major issues that have tarnished the image of Islam over the past decade. Between the misconceptions held by the West and a number of erroneous beliefs held by Muslims, many of Islam's beliefs have been misconstrued and misrepresented. We must acknowledge that these misconceptions exist.

It must also be recognized that understanding Islam by way of the *Quran* is an extremely difficult task for a number of reasons. First, the *Quran* is written in the form of poetry and therefore the reader must consider the format, language, tone, emotion, and imagery used; in other words, one cannot understand the *Quran* through a literal reading of the text. Second, the *ayahs* (verses) within the *Quran* were revealed in respect to very specific events. Therefore the *Quran* requires an understanding of the historical events that took place during the revelation of these *ayahs*. Lastly, some verses also require the *ahadith* for proper interpretation. One example that conveys the complexity of the *Quran* is in the first *surah* (chapter), *al-fatiha*. Regarded by many as the most important *surah*, *al-fatiha* is composed of only seven verses and is made up of twenty-nine words yet their exists well over fifty different translations.

The *Quran* itself offers some words on the complexity of its interpretations. *Surah* 3:7 states: "It is He Who has revealed the Book to you. Some of its verses are absolutely clear and lucid, and these are the core of the Book. Others are ambiguous." It is for this reason that scholars have placed the *ayahs* of the *Quran* into two categories – some verses are *mukham* while others are *mutashabih*. *Mukham* are those *ayahs* whose meaning is clear and easy to understand, requiring little to no interpretation. The other *ayahs* are called *mutashabih*, which can appear ambiguous and often in the form of allegory. These *ayahs* are more complicated in their meanings and require a more in-depth analysis to reveal their inner truths.

It is absolutely essential that readers of this book understand the level of difficulty towards understanding the *Quran*. In 2010, British-American writer and author Lesley Hazleton addressed this very issue during her appearance on TED Talks titled "On Reading the *Quran*" and said:

> Part of the problem I think is that we imagine that the *Quran* can be read as we usually read a book – as though we can curl up with it on a rainy afternoon with a bowl of popcorn within reach as though God – and the *Quran* is entirely in the voice of God speaking to *Muhammad* – were just another author on the bestseller list. Yet the fact that so few people do actually read the

Quran is precisely why it's so easy to quote, that is, to misquote. Phrases and snippets taken out of context in what I call the highlighter version, which is one favored by both Muslim fundamentalists and anti-Muslim Islamophobes.

It should also be noted that while I have a modest degree of knowledge about the Islamic faith, it is by no means extensive and the conclusions reached in this book should neither be regarded as absolute truths nor substitutions for all forms of religious authority. The aim of this book is not to pass decree but rather to tackle common questions and misconceptions regarding the Western and the Muslim worlds' perceptions of Islam using logic and reason. If nothing else, I hope this book can contribute to the discussion on Islamophobia and help pave the way towards a more tolerant and accepting society.

Part One – Muntik Arrives

The Return of Muntik

As I peered out the window, my heart began to race. The eastern light broke free from its nightly hibernation, dissipating the darkness that had spread across the land. Once the night had been cast out, the gates around the capital were opened. Soon, moving bodies overtook the entire city. Clouds of dust hovered over the city as the footsteps of the masses shook the earth. From all across the land, many had journeyed to see what should have occurred long ago. It was time for the damage to be undone.

Some of the spectators belonged to the Uhuru Pk tribe who had travelled from high above the earth, from near the skies – these were the Mountain People. Behind the Uhuru Pk were the Owami who journeyed across the waterless land – these were the Desert People. Behind the Owami were the Jubba who came from the low lands – these were the Valley People. Behind the Jubba were the Kuiseb who crossed the water – these were the River People. Behind the Kuiseb were the Mauritius who left their isolated habitat – these were the Island People. There were many more who had left their homes to witness this great spectacle. By sunrise, the entire city had migrated to the town square like a group of worker bees swarming towards their hive to protect their queen from harm.

I quickly sprang up from the floor and hurled myself through the door. I ran towards the town square as fast as my legs would allow. Being four feet tall, I could not afford to witness the event from afar. I dashed through the crowd avoiding the barrage of swaying arms and used my thin frame to crawl through the thousands of shuffling legs.

Completely out of breath and coated with dust, I gazed at the town square. Waiting at the center were the three-cloaked men – these were the *Motheyeen*.

Father told me that these men were responsible for most of the mischief in our land. Through their treachery and their deceit, the

Motheyeen were able to lead my people away from their lives of virtue and justice and into one filled with ancestral contempt, wickedness, and falsehood. When I asked father where the *Motheyeen* had come from, he answered they had always been a part of us. It was only recently that they had succeeded in casting their spells of deceit amongst our people. Over time they had grown more powerful and today they have become a prominent force.

This is my father's story: "Though the *Motheyeen* have always lived within this land, their power of influence only recently gained new heights. In their weakest of times, the *Motheyeen* had virtually no control over our people. Despite their strongest efforts to disrupt the harmony of the city through their rhetoric and hypocrisy, we held firm to our ancestors' beliefs. Yet as the fortunes granted to us wither with time, so too, does the strength of man. Soon, misfortune befell us all and we were alone, left without a leader to rule the land. Without warning, the *Motheyeen* descended upon their unknowing victims and managed to seize control of this land's greatest strength – the minds of the people. The *Motheyeen* swept through our homes, offering to be our protectors. Many blindly accepted their false promises of deliverance – desperation is one of the many roots that make up the tree of weakness.

"The *Motheyeen* had succeeded in manipulating our people to accept a perverted version of our faith. Soon the way of our ancestors became a distant memory. A small group of us banded together and vowed to restore truth to our land. Despite our strongest efforts, we failed to open their eyes. Our people had forsaken the way of our ancestors and instead embraced the false light of the *Motheyeen*. Regrettably, even our own perseverance in fighting the *Motheyeen's* influence began to diminish, just as a candle struggles to stay lit as its source of oxygen runs low. I soon found myself standing alone, left with no friend or kin to comfort me. I considered joining the masses but thought better than to betray my faith and ancestors – loneliness is a dangerously persuasive friend.

"Unable to contain myself any longer, I prepared for the losing battle. I approached the *Motheyeen* in the town square armed with my helmet of honor, armor of pride, and my sword of truth. And so it began. As I spoke in favor of the ways of the past, the *Motheyeen* rebuked me and argued against our ancestral traditions; is change not the ingredient of success, they would ask. With no strength other than my unwavering faith, I accepted what I knew I could no longer prolong – defeat. Left without pride, I fled the land whose air had once entered my mouth only to deliver to my lungs what was my first breath.

"Over the next ten years, I lived a life of solitude owning nothing more than a broken heart, still yearning for the restoration of my ancestors' traditions. My health began to wither and I feared my faith would soon follow. As I flirted with the darkness of submission, a light came in the shape of a man.

"There was nothing particularly special about this man. His stature was average and his appearance ordinary but it was when he spoke that my soul was put at ease – hope had not forsaken us. His voice was soft and his speech elegant; his words rich, yet simple. His name was *Muntik*.

"*Muntik* was aware of the *Motheyeen* and their trail of deceit; in fact it was their treachery that had brought *Muntik* towards our land. Eager to avenge the honor of our ancestors, I offered to take him to the *Motheyeen*. To my disappointment, *Muntik* declined my request and said he would make the journey himself when the time was right. Having given me his word that he will right the wrong done by the *Motheyeen*, I revisited the land that I called home."

This was my father's favorite story. It was the only tale that filled him with hope. I was certain that it was all a dream, a vision that he had created to cope with his depression. At last, the day had finally arrived for the mysterious man from my father's story to cast away the darkness and restore the traditions of our ancestors.

We had all gathered around the town square, awaiting the presence of the only savior our land would ever see. *Muntik* was still nowhere to be seen – I began to wonder if his coming was a lie. Were my father's stories just stories? Did my father really invent this man out of desperation?

The sun was at its zenith and *Muntik* had still not arrived. My heart sank deep within my chest. Suddenly I heard shouts resonating from behind. After a few moments, a shadowy figure emerged – he had arrived. *Muntik* was exactly as father described him; there was nothing glorious about him. No marks of outstanding beauty, no great stature or anything of the sort. He stood wrapped in a white cloak, sitting on top of an Arabian horse. Unlike its rider, the mare embodied perfection. Its gallop was swift, its stride graceful. Its body enveloped with thick white hair that gleamed from the sun's rays.

In the center were the *Motheyeen*, the three-cloaked men. Their names were *Kazab*, *Sooilfahim*, and *Sakheef*. Facing them was *Muntik*. Surrounding them were the people of the land and of the lands beyond.

It was time for the great debate.

Muntik's Message

"As the Prophet Jesus once said: 'Do not think that I have come to abolish the Law.'[xv] I am here merely to right what has been wronged. The day came when you were left without a leader, and thus guidance. Seized with fear, you opened your hearts to those you did not trust. You were blinded by desperation, paralyzed by fear, and frightened by uncertainty.

"I ask you: Have you no dignity that you sell your soul to the devil and forsake the way of your ancestors? You have lived under the rule of the *Motheyeen* for so long that you have become like the chained prisoner, accustomed to a freedom-less life and unwilling to leave.

"You have lived in the shadow of falsehood for far too long. It is time to cast away the darkness of the midnight sky, clear away the clouds and let the sun's rays shine throughout the land.

"I realize that one of the hardest things a person can do is to question their own beliefs. To fill with doubt what the heart has accepted to be true is no easy task. Even if the mind is convinced, the human heart holds onto personal beliefs like an infant clings to its mother's breast. I ask that you peel away the layers of falsehood that encapsulates your heart.

"Do not let my words be wasted on you. I realize that I am but a stranger to your land with no friend or kin from among you all. Trust that I am to your soul what a cloud is to a field of flowers – allow me to water your gardens with life and sustenance. The human soul flourishes under honesty and moral righteousness. It is for this reason I ask that you reflect on your present beliefs for they are filled with deceit, falsehood, and dishonesty. I do not wish for you to reject these beliefs based on nothing but my words. To do so would fail to break the cycle of blind acceptance.

"People of this land, let logic and reason serve as the masters of your mind and virtue the dweller of your soul. Break the chains that hold your heart captive. Allow the truth to flow freely through your veins. The most important asset of a land is its people; the failure and weakness of one man or one woman is felt through the bones of all.

"Do not fear change; embrace it. Do not travel backwards; move forward. Do not return to your caves of solitude; come out into the shining light. Let the sun's warmth fill your body with strength and let my words guide your souls. Let your ancestors' traditions flourish as they once did.

"Free yourselves."

Part Two – Muntik versus the Motheyeen

Taqiyya and its Limits

A man from the crowd yelled: "Speak to him of how Islam commands Muslims to deceive others and then kill them!"

"*Muntik*, how can you come here defending a faith which commands its followers to lie and then kill anyone whose beliefs are different than their own?" said *Kazab*.

"I am unaware of any such command."

"Do you deny that *taqiyya* is an Islamic concept that allows Muslims to lie to non-Muslims without restriction?"

"While I cannot deny that *taqiyya* is an Islamic concept, I must refute this notion that it allows Muslims to lie to non-Muslims without restriction. Tell me *Kazab*, what is *taqiyya*?"

"I have already told you. It is a doctrine that allows Muslims to lie to non-Muslims without boundaries. This is even supported in *surah* 16, *ayah* 106!"

"Not quite. T*aqiyya*[1] is not to be used when one is merely under pressure but rather when one is facing persecution. There is a great difference between being pressured and having a knife placed against your throat, would you not agree? Second, *taqiyya* is not simply lying to protect your religion but to protect yourself from physical or mental harm.[2] *Kazab*, do you understand the historical context behind this concept?"

---

[1] Simply speaking, *taqiyya* refers to dissimulation, i.e. not being forthright with one's faith.

[2] Some critics of Islam assert that *taqiyya* is an Islamic concept that encourages Muslims to deceive and betray non-Muslims in order to spread Islam. By accepting *taqiyya* as a doctrine of treachery against non-Muslims, critics have essentially convicted Muslims without trial. How can a Muslim ever acquit *taqiyya* of such charges when anything a Muslim says will just be labeled as misleading in practice? At this point, proper debate becomes virtually impossible. If one accepts the position that *taqiyya* is a strategy allowing Muslims to lie about anything to non-Muslims, then wouldn't any Muslims' discussion on *taqiyya* – and anything else – to non-Muslims be considered flawed from the start?

"I do not," replied *Kazab*.

"As you can imagine, when the Prophet *Muhammad* began preaching the existence of One God and the importance of charity and helping the poor, the *Quraysh* were quite unhappy. The *Quraysh* were a wealthy and powerful *Meccan* tribe who believed in polytheism and paganism. Threatened by the growing popularity of the Prophet *Muhammad*, the *Quraysh* sought to solidify their influence and began torturing and killing his followers. One notable sufferer was *Ammar bin Yasir*, a beloved and loyal companion of the Prophet *Muhammad*. *Ammar* and his parents all converted to Islam. Upon this news *Abu Jahl*, one of the most prominent and hostile *Quraysh* leaders, led a group of *Meccan* polytheists to *Ammar's* house. After torching it down, they took *Ammar*, his mother *Summayya* and his father *Yasir* to a desert outside of *Mecca*. At first, they were whipped and had heavy rocks placed upon their chests as the sun beat down on them. When *Abu Jahl* and his followers returned later that day, he asked *Summayya* if she would renounce her faith in Islam and accept the idols as her Gods, but she refused. *Summayya* reaffirmed her faith in the God of Islam. Enraged, *Abu Jahl* thrust his spear into her belly, killing *Summayya*. It is for this reason that *Summayya* is considered the first martyr of Islam. Unfortunately, her husband *Yasir* met the same fate. Filled with fear and terror, *Ammar* renounced his belief in Islam and praised the Pagan Gods. It is important to realize *Kazab* that *Ammar* did not actually believe in the Pagan Gods. He only claimed to in order to avoid death – his heart was still with Islam. When *Ammar* relayed the story, the Prophet *Muhammad* asked him: 'How do you feel about this, in your heart?' *Ammar* replied: 'My heart is fully convinced of the faith [Islam].' In response, the Prophet *Muhammad* said: 'If they put you to the same torture again, you may utter the same words.' It is this incident that the *Quran* is referring to in *surah* 16, *ayah* 106:

> Except for those who were forced to engage in infidelity to Allah after believing the while their hearts remained firmly convinced of their belief, the ones whose hearts willingly embraced disbelief shall incur Allah's wrath and a mighty chastisement lies in store for them. [xvi]

This, *Kazab*, was the earliest use of *taqiyya* in Islam. Another prominent example of the use of *taqiyya* occurred during the reign of *Al-Mansur*, the second *caliph* of the *Abbasid* dynasty. Under his rule, he ordered the persecution of *Shia* Muslims. In order to avoid persecution, *Shias* would deny their belief in Shiism."

"Enough *Muntik*! What kind of a religion tells its followers to renounce their faith?"

"To deny is not the same as to renounce. Even this denial is nothing but a verbal refutation of an inner truth:

> 'If any one is compelled and professes unbelief with his tongue, while his heart contradicts him, to escape his enemies, no blame falls on him, because God takes his servants as their hearts believe.'[xvii]

In fact, the *Quran* even refers to one of Pharaoh's people who had, until that moment, concealed his faith in the Prophet Moses from the Pharaoh:

> Then a man endowed with faith, from Pharaoh's folk, who had kept his faith hidden, said: "Do you kill a person simply because he says: 'My Lord is Allah' even though he brought to you clear Signs from your Lord?[xviii]

Now *Kazab*, this idea of denying one's faith to avoid persecution is not uniquely Islamic. Are you familiar with crypto-Christians and crypto-Jews?"

"I am not," answered *Kazab*.

"Crypto-Christianity and crypto-Judaism refer to the secret practice of Christianity and Judaism. Just as the early Muslims denied their faith from their persecutors, Christians during the early years of Christianity under the Roman Empire also practiced their faith in secret for fear of persecution. Similar, crypto-Jews publically adhered to non-Judaic faiths while secretly practicing Judaism. Why do you charge Muslims with wrongful doing but lay no blame on Jews and Christians when they have done the same? *Taqiyya* is nothing more than concealing your faith in order to avoid physical or mental harm. Anything outside of this domain is not *taqiyya* and any further comparisons should be tossed aside."³

---

³ *Taqiyya* is strictly limited to situations where professing one's faith may result in great danger or harm to the individual. Anything beyond these limits does not fall within the acceptable boundaries of *taqiyya*.

The Islamic View on Women

A woman from the crowd yelled: "Speak to him of Islam's insubordinate view of women!"

"There is no denying this truth, *Muntik*. The *Quran* and the *ahadith* are filled with degrading words against women," said *Kazab*.

"You charge Islam with a most serious crime, though I am confident that this is another misunderstanding," said *Muntik* reassuringly.

"How blinded you are by hope. Come, defend Islam's commandment for husbands to beat their wives. The *Quran* clearly says:

> Men are the protectors and maintainers of women because Allah has made one of them excel over the other[4], and because they spend out of their possessions (to support them). Thus righteous women are obedient and guard the rights of men in their absence under Allah's protection. As for women of whom you fear rebellion, admonish them, and remain apart from them in beds, and beat them. Then if they obey you, do not see ways to harm them. Allah is Exalted, Great.[xix]

Have you nothing to say?"

"A great deal, actually. According to this *ayah*, what should a husband do if he fears his wife will not respect and guard his rights?"

"Why, he should urge his wife to do so," replied *Kazab*.

"And if the problem persists?"

"They should remain apart in bed."

"Yes. And lastly?"

"To beat them," said *Kazab* with a smile across his face.

---

[4] It is noteworthy to mention that the words "Allah has made one of them excel over the other" do not imply that males have a superior honor or dignity over women. Rather, it is stating that men have specific qualities that make them capable of being "protectors and maintainers."

"*Kazab*, what is the Arabic word that the *Quran* uses when you refer to beating?"

"I do not know."

"Then allow me to tell you. The word in Arabic is *adriboo*, the root of which is *daraba*. I hope you recognize that this word is used in more places within the *Quran* than just this *ayah* and in varying contexts. Sometimes *daraba* means to beat, to strike to separate, to condemn, or even to part."[5]

"What are you implying, *Muntik*?"

"I am merely demonstrating how the same root word in Arabic can take on a number of different meanings, though this context can be lost in translation. In fact, *daraba* is used else where in the same *surah* as the *ayah* you provided:

> Beleivers! When you go forth in the way of Allah, discern (between friend and foe), and do not say to him who offers you the greeting of peace: 'You are not a believer.' If you seek the good of this worldly life, there lies with Allah abundant gain. After all, you too were such before, and then Allah was gracious to you. Discern, then, for Allah is well aware of what you do.[xx]

In this instance, the word *daraba* means 'to go forth,' or 'to go abroad,' or 'to leave.' Many scholars use this translation when interpreting *surah* 4, *ayah* 34. Therefore, this *ayah* reads that if a husband and wife cannot resolve their dispute, then as a final step the couple should undergo a further degree of separation where they are to temporarily remain apart from each other. In treating your wives, the Prophet *Muhammad* once said:

> I went to the Apostle of Allah and asked him: What do you say about our wives? He replied: Give them food what you have for

---

[5] There are literally dozens of *ayah*s where the word *daraba* is seen in the *Quran*, often with different meanings. *Surah* 2, *ayah* 26 states: "Behold! Allah is not ashamed to propound the parable of a gnat, or even of something more lowly." In this example, *daraba* is translated to mean propound. *Surah* 2, *ayah* 61 states: "And ignominy and wretchedness were pitched upon them and they were laden with the burden of Allah's wrath." Here, *daraba* is translated to laden. Lastly, *surah* 2, *ayah* 273 states: "Those needy ones who are wholly wrapped up in the cause of Allah, and who are hindered from moving about the earth in search of their livelihood, especially deserve help." In this *ayah*, *daraba* is translated into moving.

yourself, and clothe them by which you clothe yourself, and do not beat them, and do not revile them.[xxi]

What other questions do you have for me *Kazab*?"

"Perhaps the *Quran* does not call for husbands to beat their wives, but I assure you there are many other examples demonstrating Islam's contempt for women."

"Then do not keep me waiting."

"There is a *hadith* that declares women to be deficient in faith:

> It is narrated on the authority of 'Abdullah b. Umar that the Messenger of Allah observed: O womenfolk, you should give charity and ask much forgiveness for I saw you in bulk amongst the dwellers of Hell. A wise lady among them said: Why is it, Messenger of Allah, that our folk is in bulk in Hell? Upon this the Holy Prophet observed: You curse too much and are ungrateful to your spouses. I have seen none lacking in common sense and failing in religion but (at the same time) robbing the wisdom of the wise, besides you. Upon this the woman remarked: What is wrong with our common sense and with religion? He (the Holy Prophet) observed: Your lack of common sense (can be well judged from the fact) that the evidence of two women is equal to one man, that is a proof of the lack of common sense, and you spend some nights (and days) in which you do not offer prayer and in the month of Ramadan (during the days) you do not observe fast, that is a failing in religion.[xxii]

If that is not enough, let us not forget that women under Islam only receive a portion of the inheritance that men do. What is your defense?"

"You have made many accusations *Kazab*. The first is that women are deficient in faith, as demonstrated through their abstaining from prayer and fasting during when in a state of menstruation. The second is their intellectual inferiority, as demonstrated by the fact that two women are needed for one man when bearing witness to testimony. The final point is that women are worth less than men, as demonstrated through the ruling that a female is to receive only a portion of the inheritance that a male receives. Is this correct?"

"Precisely."

"Excellent. Let us go through each of these points separately."

"Very well," said *Kazab*.

"The first point is that women are deficient in faith due to menstruation. In Islam, women are forbidden from praying, fasting, and directly touching the *Quran* with their hands during menstruation. The *Quran* states:

> No! I swear by the positions of the stars – and this is indeed a mighty oath, if only you knew – that this indeed is a noble Qu'ran inscribed in a well-guarded Book, which none but the pure may touch; a revelation from the Lord of the Universe.[xxiii]

Do you know why this is?"

"I do not," said *Kazab*.

"You see *Kazab*, the *Quran* instructs its followers to only touch the *Quran* when in a state of purity and cleanliness. Put another way, in order to pray, fast, or touch the *Quran*, Muslims cannot be in a state of impurity.[6] When a woman is menstruating, she is not in a state of purity or cleanliness and is therefore told to abstain from these acts. This is not by any means a punishment and should not be regarded as a disadvantageous state. These rules are merely illustrating the holiness and sanctity of prayer and fasting. Now as for your argument that a woman's menstruation cycle leads to a deficiency in faith, I see three reasons why this is not so."

"I will be the judge of that."

"Did God create men and women to be deficient?"

"Of course not. We are the makers of our own deficiencies."

"So you would agree that we alone are responsible for our deficiencies?"

"Absolutely. Who else is to blame?"

"But what about deficiencies that are out of our control? For you see *Kazab*, a woman does not choose when to menstruate. In fact, one may argue that it is God who created women with this biological process. Or am I mistaken?"

---

[6] Muslims are forbidden from praying, fasting, or touching the *Quran* if in a state of impurity. In Islam, one is considered impure for these activities if they are menstruating, actively bleeding, or having released bodily fluids. To be in a state of purity, Muslims are required to wash their bodies; in respect to bleeding, staunching the blood flow is all that is required.

"No *Muntik*, you are correct. Women have no control over it."

"So it would appear that menstruation is a deficiency from God?"

"It would appear so."

"But did we not just agree that God did not create men and women to be deficient?"

"I was mistaken before. I believe God does create men and women to be deficient," said *Kazab*.

"In that case, does God expect more piety between one person and another?"

"Of course not."

"I would agree with you. The *Quran* makes this point when it says:

> Whoever does good and believes – whether he is male or female – such shall enter the Garden, and they shall not be wronged in the slightest.[xxiv]

> Whosoever acts righteously – whether a man or a woman – and embraces belief, We will surely grant him a good life; and will surely grant such persons their reward according to the best of their deeds.[xxv]

> Whosoever does an evil deed will be requited only with the like of it; and whosoever acts righteously and has attained to faith be he a male or a female they shall enter Paradise and be provided sustenance beyond all reckoning.[xxvi]

Tell me Kazab, if menstruation results in a deficiency in faith, wouldn't women have to perform more acts of piety in order to attain the same level of piety as men?"

"It would seem so."

"But did we not just agree that God does not expect more piety from one person to another? In fact the *Quran* states:

> Their Lord answered the Prayer thus: "I will not suffer the work of any of you, whether male or female, to go to waste; each of you is from the other."[xxvii]

According to this *ayah*, in the eyes of God we are all equal. Both men and women are judged by the same criteria."

"Enough of this *Muntik*. Your words are more confusing than they are convincing."

"Then allow me to move onto my second rebuttal. Tell me, what constitutes religious faith?"

"Why a lot of things, *Muntik*."

"If you pray, can that represent faith?"

"Yes."

"And what about fasting?"

"Fasting as well."

"And reading the *Quran*?"

"The *Quran* also."

"Giving to the poor?"

"Yes."

"Proclaiming God's existence?"

"Yes."

"And what about virtuous actions? Could they represent faith?"

"Religion tells us to be virtuous *Muntik*, so yes virtuous actions can also represent faith."

"Helping someone in need?

"Certainly."

"Would you not also agree that sometimes an individual who is lacking in their religious duties of prayer and fasting though abundant in their acts of virtue and righteousness is sometimes better than a person who is lacking in virtue and righteousness though abundant in prayer and fasting?"

"Yes, of course," said *Kazab*.

"*Kazab*, which of these displays of faith can not be performed during a woman's menstruation?"

"Fasting, prayer, and touching the *Quran*."

"This leaves us with much to work with! A woman in menstruation can still give to charity, proclaim God's existence, be virtuous, help those in need and much more. Would you agree?"

"I do," said *Kazab* reluctantly.

"And did we not also agree that prayer and fasting are not the only displays of faith, that virtuous and righteous behavior are also acts of faith?"

"We did."

"You see *Kazab*, faith is not confined to acts of prayer and fasting. The *ahadith* stating that women are deficient in faith because they have to abstain from certain religious duties during menstruation bears no weight considering there are a number of other ways that faith can be displayed. One might also argue that having these extra days when women must abstain from praying gives them time to reflect – a pastime that could increase their faith even more. And now we arrive at the third reason causing me to doubt these *ahadith's* legitimacy. When does Islam require a Muslim to begin praying and fasting?"

"Upon reaching puberty," answered *Kazab*.

"And who reaches puberty first, boys or girls?"

"Girls."

"Which would imply that women, on average, end up praying and fasting a few years before men do. Is this correct?"

"It is."

"Well if you wish to define one's level of faith and piety by their prayers and fasts, could one not argue that having those extra years of prayer and fasting provides women with even more faith and piety than men?" I see we are still not convinced. *Kazab*, is the exemption from prayer and fasting optional?"

"No it is mandatory."

"Then how can any *hadith* assert that obeying religious command is a failing in faith? Isn't abstaining from prayer and fasting an example of abiding by religious law, and therefore a display of faith?"[7]

"*Muntik* you have made your point. Women may not be deficient in faith, but in intellect it is certain!

---

[7] There are scholars who believe that Islam exempts menstruating women from fasting not because they are in a state of impurity, but rather as a mercy. Some women have more debilitating menses than others making their fast increasingly more difficult and uncomfortable. Fasting in these conditions would be an unfair burden. It is also for this reason that Islam forbids Muslims from fasting if they are sick or traveling. The Quran addresses this issue in *surah* 2, *ayah* 286: "Allah does not lay a responsibility on anyone beyond his capacity." The reason why the exemption is mandatory is so that individuals in those more vulnerable states do not feel guilty or pressured to fast.

> Believers! Whenever you contract a debt from one another for a known term, commit it to writing. Let a scribe write it down between you justly, and the scribe may not refuse to write it down according to what Allah has taught him; so let him write, and let the debtor dictate; and let him fear Allah, his Lord, and curtail no part of it. If the debtor be feebleminded, weak, or incapable of dictating, let his guardian dictate equitably, and call upon two of your men as witnesses; but if two men are not there, then let there be one man and two women as witnesses from among those acceptable to you so that if one of the two women should fail to remember, the other might remind her. Let not the witnesses refuse when they are summoned (to give evidence). Do not show slackness in writing down the transaction, whether small or large, along with the term of its payment. That is fairest in the sight of Allah; it is best for testimony and is more likely to exclude all doubts. If it be a matter of buying and selling on the spot, it is not blameworthy if you do not write it down; but do take witnesses when you settle commercial transactions with one another. And the scribe or the witness may be done no harm. It will be sinful if you do so. Beware of the wrath of Allah. He teaches you the Right Way and has full knowledge of everything.[xxviii]

You cannot deny that the *Quran* requires two female witnesses for one male witness."

"*Kazab*, what do you know of purchasing a horse?"

"What an odd question *Muntik*. Not very much."

"And of a horse's well-being, can you tell whether one is healthy or ill?"

"I would not be able to tell."

"What about your neighbor *Kazab*, does he know anything of the like? Does he know the trade of purchasing horses?"

"My neighbor is as ignorant as I am."

"Should you decide to purchase a horse, what would you do?"

"I would certainly have an expert on horses do my bidding."

"If you could not find such an expert, would you go alone?"

"Not unless I wish to be taken for a fool. I would bring my neighbor with me."

"The same neighbor whose knowledge on horses is equal to yours?"

"Two minds are better than one."

"*Kazab*, I believe you have just resolved this issue for the both of us! It is imperative to understand that this *ayah* is specifically referring to financial matters. Remember that the *Quran* was written well over 1000 years ago in the context of, by and large, a patriarchal society. It was a society where men took charge of virtually all business and financial transactions. Generally, women were neither trained nor largely involved in finance and other matters of business.[8] As a result, the *Quran* stated that as witnesses, two women with some knowledge within that field would serve as an appropriate substitute to a single male with full knowledge of it.[9] This is the same conclusion that you came up with, that if you could not find an expert who has full knowledge you and your neighbor would suffice since you each have some knowledge. Now, let us remove any further doubts that may still exist. The *Quran* says:

> As for those who accuse their wives (of unchastity), and have no witnesses except themselves: the testimony of such a one is that he testify, swearing by Allah four times, that he is truthful (in his accusation), and a fifth time, that the curse of Allah be on him if he by lying (in his accusation). And the punishment shall be averted from the woman if she were to testify, swearing by Allah four times that the man was lying, and a fifth time that the wrath of Allah be on her if the man be truthful (in his accusation).[xxix]

---

[8] In Pre-Islamic Mecca, the majority of women did not take part in matters of business. However, this is not to say that women were completely excluded. Khadija, the Prophet *Muhammad*'s first wife, had inherited her father's wealth and later became a prominent businesswoman in her own right. Thus, while most women were often excluded from the business sphere, their involvement was not unheard of.

[9] Does this algorithm of witnesses continue to apply in a modern-world where women are equally educated and capable of understanding matters of finance and business as men are? Many scholars argue that the teachings of the *Quran* are timeless and therefore inherently apply to all societies. A scholar who challenges this notion is Nasr Abu Zayd, a late Egyptian *Quranic* thinker and liberal theologian. While Abu Zayd does not deny that the *Quran* is of divine origin, he argues against a single interpretation and rather favors a multidimensional interpretation of the text. According to Abu Zayd, an absolute understanding of the *Quran* can never be attained considering each reader of the text has their own cultural and social beliefs that will inevitable be introduced into its interpretation. It is not difficult to extend this philosophy of thought to also include the need to reinterpret certain *Quranic ayah*s whose contextual foundation is 7th century Arabia. It is essential that such an approach not be perceived as a means of reinterpreting the *Quran* in its entirety. Rather, it is only meant to highlight that certain teachings of the *Quran* that were influenced by specific events and societal norms may no longer be applicable in today's society.

This *ayah* clearly equates the testimony of a single male witness to that of a single female witness. Nevertheless, there are matters whereby a woman's testimony alone is sufficient, such as in matters pertaining to birth. As you can see, there are certain situations where a man's testimony is more suitable than a woman's testimony and vice versa. I hope I have fairly demonstrated that Islam does not unanimously and universally value a male's testimony over a female's."

"You have only dealt with half of my charges."

"Then do not let me hold you back *Kazab*."

"Very well. There is clear proof that the overall value of women is less than that of men:

> Allah thus commands you concerning your children: the share of the male is like that of two females. If (the heirs of the deceased are) more than two daughters, they shall have two-thirds of the inheritance; and if there is only one daughter, then she shall have half the inheritance. If the deceased has any offspring, each of his parents shall have a sixth of the inheritance; and if the deceased has no child and his parents alone inherit him, then one-third shall go to his mother; and if the deceased has brothers and sisters, then one-sixth shall go to his mother. All these shares are to be given after payment of the bequest he might have made or any debts outstanding against him. You do not know which of them, your parents or your children, are more beneficial to you. But these portions have been determined by Allah, for He indeed knows all, is cognizant of all beneficent considerations. And to you belongs half of whatever has been left behind by your wives if they die childless; but if they have any children then to you belongs a fourth of what they have left behind, after payment of the bequest they might have made or any debts outstanding against them. And to them belongs a fourth of what you leave behind, if you die childless; and if you have any child then to them belongs one-eighth of what you have left behind, after the payment of the bequest you might have made or any debts outstanding against you. And if the man or woman has no heir in the direct line, but has a brother or sister, then each of these shall inherit one-sixth; but if they are more than two, then they shall inherit one-third of the inheritance, after the payment of the bequest that might have been made or any debts outstanding against the deceased, providing that the bequest causes no injury. This is a commandment from Allah; Allah is All-Knowing, All-Forbearing.[xxx]

How can you believe that Islam values men and women equally when a woman's share of inheritance is less than that of a man?"

"Allow me to shed some light on this matter.[10] There are three reasons why a male receives a greater inheritance than a female. Tell me *Kazab*, according to Islamic law does a man give a woman a dowry[11] or does the woman give a man a dowry?

"You had it right the first time, *Muntik*. It is the man who gives the woman her dowry."

"What about allowance? In Islamic law is it the wife who provides allowance to the husband, or is it the husband who provides allowance to the wife?"

"It is the husband who is required to provide."

"And whose responsibility is it to provide food and take care of the family?"

"It is the husband."

"Let us not forget that the husband has no right to touch any of his wife's money without her permission. So let us summarize. According to Islamic law, the husband is obligated to pay a dowry, to provide an allowance, and is responsible for all financial obligations of the household. This is not to say that a wife cannot contribute or even take on all financial obligations. These laws were implemented with the intent of protecting the wealth of women. With this in mind *Kazab*, on who would you say the financial burden lies? Is it the husband or the wife?"

"It is the husband."

"If this is the case, why would you give each of your children an equal amount of inheritance if your son will need more than your daughter? If it is your son, and not your daughter, who will be

---

[10] There are specific criteria and rules of allocation regarding the distribution of inheritance. While there are circumstances where a son receives twice the inheritance of a daughter, there are also situations where inheritance is distributed equally. For example, the father and mother of a deceased each receive one-sixth the inheritance if the deceased has at least one child.

[11] Dowry is a practice where the husband provides an offering, usually in money or property to the bride or her family upon marriage. In Pre-Islamic Arabia, dowry went to the bride's family. Islam reformed this practice and instead mandated that the dowry go directly to the bride.

responsible for all financial expenses associated with marriage and a family, do you not think he should receive a larger portion of inheritance?"

"I would," said *Kazab* reluctantly.

"Come now, what other charges do you bring forward?" said *Muntik*.

"Islam allows its people to rape their female slaves[12], as demonstrated in *surah* 23 of the *Quran*:

> The believers have indeed attained true success: those who, in their Prayers, humble themselves; who avoid whatever is vain and frivolous; who observe Zakat; who strictly guard their private parts save from their wives, or those whom their right hands possess; for with regard to them they are free from blame.[xxxi]

Surely you are lost for words *Muntik*."

"A heavy accusation you have made *Kazab*! Allow me to address it at once so that I may alleviate the burden you have laid upon our chests."

"By all means," smirked *Kazab*.

"It is widely regarded that those whom your 'right hand possess' refers to men and women taken as slaves during times of war. As you know, the life of prisoners of war is not an envious one. In fact their fate is one of cruelty and is often inhumane.[13] Now please keep in mind that this discussion is not an easy one to have. This space where prisoners of war, prostitution, and concubines

---

[12] Some critics of Islam argue that the *Quran* and the *ahadith* not only justify sexual slavery, but also encourage it. These critics take it one step further by asserting that Muslims are even allowed to rape their slaves.

[13] The grim reality surrounding prisoners of war and the possibility of forced prostitution and rape is unfortunately a common one. In the 1940s, Nazi Germany established brothels within concentration camps where women captives were forced into prostitution in hopes that it would enhance productivity and collaboration among male prisoners.[I] More recently in 2015, Shinzo Abe, the prime minister of Japan, agreed to pay one billion yen to South Korea in reparations for the forced prostitution and sexual assault of South Korean women during World War II. Known as comfort women (a euphemism for the Japanese word Ifan, which means prostitute), around 200,000 women were sexually enslaved by Japan and forced into sex trade.[II]

intersect is an ugly one and is an area that Islam did not create but rather sought to reform.[14]

"Enlighten us all about this reformation *Muntik*," said *Kazab* mockingly.

"Very well. In its most basic form, Islam requires its observers to do no injustice to one another and to partake in the five pillars. The *Quran* and *ahadith* also offer recommendations on actions that are not compulsory but that are regarded as virtuous. This also applies to prisoners of war. At the very least, Muslims are to cause no harm or injustice against them. What does Islam recommend when dealing with these prisoners? Why, it asks Muslims to free <u>them and to ultimately help them</u> reintegrate into society. Islam even

[14] While it may seem obvious, it is imperative to recognize that Islam did not create or introduce concepts such as slavery or concubines into its environment. In fact before the advent of Islam in Arabia, slavery and polygamy had essentially no boundaries; a man could have as many wives and concubines as he wished, and a master held immeasurable authority over his slave. During its rise, Islam found itself immersed in a society that was deeply enrooted in systemic slavery. Islam could not simply eradicate slavery, and instead established a method that sought to reform this system and ultimately, yet indirectly, abolish it. Therefore, in order to truly understand issues surrounding prisoners of war and slavery, one must study this area in the context of reformation. Gwyn Campbell and Elizabeth Elbourne, professors in history and co-authors of "Sex, Power and Slavery" describe Islam's role in reforming slavery: "Islam did not invent slavery, nor did it try to abolish it outright. What it tried to do was to humanize the institution through regulations and exhortations on the treatment of slaves. A slave was not merely chattel but also a human being with certain religious and legal rights and social status. Islam recognized the social reality of cohabitation with slave women and went onto explicitly acknowledge the status and rights of those women and of their offspring. It was a society governed by paternity. It permitted unions with slave girls, who became *sarari* (secondary wives, sing. *suria*) when they bore their owners' children. Thereafter, the *umm al-walad* (mother of the child) could not be sold or pawned but was freed on the death of her master (although she did not inherit from him as his free wives did). Moreover, the offspring of such unions were free children of their free fathers, with full rights like that possessed by free mothers…Manumission was thus built into the system of slavery in Islam, and it provided its own mechanisms for the assimilation of slaves into the wider fabric of the Muslim community. If offered opportunities for upward social mobility, what Ali Mazrui called 'ascending miscegenation,' in contrast to the American system, for example, in which white slave owners could not acknowledge the paternity of their children born to slave women, children who remained slaves like their mothers."

supported the marriage between an owner and a slave, thereby removing the stigma that slaves were inferior and worthless."

"You offer empty words *Muntik*," sneered *Kazab*.

"Then allow me to give them meaning. Not only do the *Quran* and the *ahadith* forbid the prostitution of slaves, but it also promotes their emancipation and reintegration into society:

> Let those who cannot afford to marry keep themselves chaste until Allah enriches them out of His Bounty. And write out a deed of manumission for such of your slaves that desire their freedom in lieu of payment - if you see any good in them - and give them out of the wealth that Allah has given you. And do not compel your slave-girls to prostitution for the sake of the benefits of worldly life the while they desire to remain chaste. And if anyone compels them to prostitution, Allah will be Most Pardoning, Much Merciful (to them) after their subjection to such compulsion.[xxxii]

> Marry those of you that are single, (whether men or women), and those of your male and female slaves that are righteous. If they are poor, Allah will enrich them out of His Bounty. Allah is Immensely Resourceful, All-Knowing.[xxxiii]

> Allah's Apostle said "Three persons will have a double reward: A Person from the people of the scriptures who believed in his prophet (Jesus or Moses) and then believed in the Prophet Muhammad (i.e. has embraced Islam). A slave who discharges his duties to Allah and his master. A master of a woman-slave who teaches her good manners and educates her in the best possible way (the religion) and manumits her and then marries her."[xxxiv]

I must mention *Kazab* that while Islam does encourage the marriage between an owner and a slave, it must be mutual. This is perhaps best illustrated with the story of *Barirah*, a slave who was wrongfully forced to marry another slave by the name of *Mughith*. *Aisha*, the daughter of *Abu Bark* and a wife of the Prophet *Muhammad*, took pity on *Barirah* and bought her freedom. Feeling that she was finally in control of her life's affair, *Barirah* decided to divorce her husband for she had not loved him. The story continues with *Mughith* running after *Barirah* with tears in his eyes begging her not to leave him. Upon witnessing this sight, the Prophet *Muhammad* went to *Barirah* and asked her 'why do you not go back to him?' *Barirah* replied, 'O Messenger of Allah, are you commanding me to do so' to which he responded, 'I am only interceding." *Barirah* simply said 'I have no need for him.' You see *Kazab*, *Barirah* was free to choose the state of her marital affairs – whether in marriage or divorce. Just imagine *Barirah,* a freed slave, rejecting the Prophet *Muhammad's* suggestion. If this does not demonstrate a woman's complete choice in matters of marriage, I do not know how else to convince you."

"What does all this matter *Muntik*? Even if a master cannot force his slave into marriage, you have done little to address the topic of intimacy with a slave."

"Then allow me *Kazab* to shine light on this matter at once.[15] Do you happen to know the criteria that must be met in order for a master to be intimate with his slave?"

"I do not."

"Then allow me to share them with you. First, if a slave's spouse is alive, whether they are free or taken captive, intimacy with that slave becomes impermissible. Second, there must be a waiting period to ensure that the slave is not pregnant, to allow them to mourn, and to give sufficient time for the slave's family to arrange for their freedom. Third, the slave cannot be in a state of negotiation for their release. Next, only one person may be intimate with the slave and that knowledge cannot be kept secret. Fifth, the slave must be of the 'people of the book'[16]. Last and most important is their must be mutual consent."[17]

---

[15] In order to promote what are regarded as virtuous deeds, the *Quran* often mentions a reward associated with those actions. For example, the *Quran* states that it will reward those believe in God (*surah* 2:62) and who pray and give to charity (*surah* 2:277). While intimacy with a slave is allowed, the *Quran* does not reward such actions. In fact, the only reward associated with slavery is either by freeing them or wedding them. This is to emphasize that the ideal goal is to free slaves and reintegrate them into society.

[16] The "people of the book" is an Islamic term used to refer to the Jews, Christians, and Sabaeans. Islam believes that each of these people received divine revelation from God and therefore are grouped together accordingly.

[17] Not only must there be consent given by the slave, but it must also be given by the slave-owner's free wife. A woman is able to stipulate in her marriage contract that should she be wed, the husband is forbidden from having intimate relations with a slave.

"And what proof do you have to offer us *Muntik* that consent is required with these slaves?"[18]

"There is a *hadith* that says:

> Zadhan Abl Umar reported: I came to Ibn 'Umar as he had granted freedom to a slave. He (the narrator further) said: He took hold of a wood or something like it from the earth and said: It (freedom of a slave) has not the reward evert equal to it, but the fact that I heard Allah's Messenger (way sallAllaahu alayhi wa sallam) say: He who slaps his slave or beats him, the expiation for it is that he should set him free.[xxxv]

If merely slapping a slave was grounds for their freedom, how can an act of rape not be seen as a far more serious crime? Perhaps you remain unconvinced. *Imam al-Shafi'i*, regarded as one of the greatest scholars in Islamic jurisprudence, addressed this issue in his book, *Kitab al-Umm*:

> If a man acquires by force a slave-girl, then has sexual intercourse with her after he acquires her by force, and if he is not excused by ignorance, then the slave-girl will be taken from him, he is required to pay the fine, and he will receive the punishment for illegal sexual intercourse.[xxxvi]

I should also add that should a child be born out of this union, then that offspring is not born a slave but is regarded as a legitimate child.[19] *Kazab*, this belief that Islam regards women as inferior to men has no strength. Do not forget many of the *ayahs* that we have discussed today come from the fourth *surah* of the *Quran*, titled *An-Nisa* (the Women). While themes of faith, justice, and one's duty to God are

---

[18] Historically, concubines are considered morganatic marriages, i.e. a marriage between two individuals of unequal social ranks. As a result, the husband's lineage, privileges, and possessions would not be passed onto his "lesser wife" or any children they bore. Traditionally, should such marriages be made public the husband would told his wife's left hand as the right hand was reserved for non-morganatic marriages. Islam reformed this area by referring to slaves as 'those whom your right hand possesses.'

[19] It was common practice that the child of a slave would also be born a slave. Not only did Islam reject this practice, but it also gave these children the opportunity to work towards freeing their enslaved parent – a right that was often only reserved for the slave-owner.

mentioned in this *surah*, it also contains many *ayahs* that speak of the rights of women, including their right to dowries, of equal inheritance, and of marriage. Let us not forget who the Prophet *Muhammad* said was the best companion:

> A man came to Allah's apostle and said: O Messenger of Allah! Who from amongst mankind warrants the best companionship from me? He replied *'Your mother.'* The man asked: *'Then who?'* So he replied: *'Your mother.'* The man then asked: Then who? So the Prophet replied again: *'Your mother.'* The man then asked: Then who? So he replied: *'Then your father.'*[xxxvii]

There are a number of *ayahs* within the *Quran* that emphasizes the idea of equality between men and women.[20] For example, unlike the other Abrahamic religions, the *Quran* does not put any blame on the weakness of women for eating from the forbidden fruit:

> But Satan made an evil suggestion to **both** of them that he might reveal to **them their** shame that had remained hidden from **them**. He said: 'Your Lord has forbidden you to approach this tree only to prevent you from becoming angels or immortals.'[xxxviii]
>
> **Both** cried out: '**Our** Lord! **We** have wronged **ourselves**. If You do not forgive **us** and do not have mercy on **us**, **we** shall surely be among the **losers**.[xxxix]

With respect to religious responsibilities, you will see that the expectations for men and women are the same:

> Surely the men who submit (to Allah) and the women who submit (to Allah) the men who have faith and the women who have faith, the men who are obedient and the women who are obedient, the men who are truthful and the women who are truthful; the men

---

[20] Not only did Islam reform the status of women but it bestowed upon them rights that Western and non-Western women did not receive until fairly recently. The Married Women's Property Act of 1882 passed by the United Kingdom gave women the right to both own and manage their property. Over half a century later, China passed the Marriage Law of 1950 granting equal status, rights, and possession of inheritance between a husband and a wife. In 1979, Louisiana became the final state to repeal a set of property laws referred to as Head and Master laws, which essentially gave husbands final authority on decisions regarding jointly owned property without the wife's consent.

who are steadfast and the women who are steadfast, the men who humble themselves (to Allah) and the women who humble themselves (to Allah), the men who give alms and the women who give alms, the men who fast and the women who fast, the men who guard their chastity and the women who guard their chastity, the men who remember Allah much and the women who remember Allah much: for them has Allah prepared forgiveness and a mighty reward.[xl,21]

Whoever does good and believes – whether he is male or female – such shall enter the Garden, and they shall not be wronged in the slightest.[xli]

Even the rewards and punishments are the same for both men and women![22] The belief that women are inferior, insubordinate, or are regarded as lesser beings than men has no place in Islam. A man who stares at a mirror sees his reflection through the eyes of a woman, just as a woman who stares at a clear stream sees her reflection through the eyes of a man."

---

[21] In a collection of *ahadith* of Imam Ahmad, it was narrated that *Umm Salama*, a wife of the Prophet *Muhammad*, asked the Prophet *Muhammad*: "O Messenger (May peace and blessings be upon him) of Allah. Why aren't we mentioned in the Quran in an equal footing with men?" It was this incident that led the Prophet *Muhammad* to reveal this *ayah* that explicitly specified the equal roles and characteristics of men and women. It would be incorrect to assume that the *Quran* did not routinely refer to women before the revelation of this *ayah*. In Arabic, words are traditionally conjugated in the male form and can simultaneously refer to both men and women; on the other hand, words conjugated in the female word traditionally refer only to women.

[22] S*urah* 5, *ayah* 38 (theft), *surah* 24, *ayah* 2 (fornication), *surah* 5, *ayah* 45 (murder and injury).

When did the Prophet Muhammad Marry Aisha?

A woman from the crowd yelled: "Speak to him of the Prophet *Muhammad's* marriage to Aisha!"

"How can you possibly defend Islam when the Prophet *Muhammad* wed *Aisha* when she was six years of age and consummated the marriage three years later," blurted *Sooilfahim*.

"I assume you base this belief on the *ahadith*?"

"How else would we gain such knowledge?"

"Then do not keep me waiting and share with me this knowledge," said *Muntik*.

"With pleasure. I shall recite only two of a handful of *ahadith* that shed light on this well-established truth:

> Narrated 'Aisha: that the Prophet married her when she was six years old and he consummated his marriage when she was nine years old, and then she remained with him for nine years (i.e., till his death).[xlii]

> Narrated 'Urwa: The Prophet wrote the (marriage contract) with 'Aisha while she was six years old and consummated his marriage with her while she was nine years old and she remained with him for nine years (i.e. till his death).[xliii]

Do you require anything else, *Muntik*?" sneered *Sooilfahim*.

"Only some more of your time. But before we continue, tell me *Sooilfahim* how long did the Prophet *Muhammad* stay in *Mecca* after receiving revelation from God?"

"For thirteen years."

"And at the time of the *hijrah*[23], the Prophet *Muhammad* was fifty-three years of age. Now do you happen to know when the Prophet *Muhammad* and *Aisha* consummated their marriage?"

---

[23] The *hijrah* refers to the journey that the Prophet *Muhammad* and his companions made from Mecca to Medina in 622 CE.

"It was during his second year in *Medina*."

"Excellent! Now that we have agreed on some basic facts, [24] I believe we can move forward on this issue," said *Muntik*.

"Very well."

"Then let us begin! First, we are told that when *surah al-Qamar* was revealed *Aisha* was a young girl. We know that *surah al-Qamar* was revealed nine years before the *hijrah*, which places the year of its revelation at 613. Now with all this in mind, I think we can begin to put things into perspective. How old would you say Aisha was at this time?"

"Well *Muntik*, I cannot say with certainty but we are told Aisha was a young child and therefore I would say she may have been around five years of age."

"And if Aisha was five in the year 613, how old would she have been at the time of the *hijrah*?"

"The *hijrah* occurred in 622 and therefore Aisha must have been thirteen years old."

"Now *Sooilfahim*, since we know that the Prophet *Muhammad* and *Aisha* consummated their marriage during the second year of the *hijrah*, this would mean that Aisha was at least fourteen years old. But perhaps you remain unconvinced. Let us try something else."[25]

"Yes I would prefer this."

"There is a *hadith* that states:

> On the day (of the battle) of Uhad when (some) people retreated and left the Prophet, I saw 'Aisha bint Abu Bakr and Um Sulaim, with their robes tucked up so that the bangles around their ankles were visible hurrying with their water skins (in another narration it is said, "carrying the water skins on their backs"). Then they would

---

[24] While the age of *Aisha* at the time of her marriage to the Prophet *Muhammad* is of much debate, it is well accepted by scholars that the Prophet *Muhammad* was fifty-three at the time of his migration to *Medina* and that he consummated his marriage to *Aisha* during his second year in *Medina*. It is also agreed that there were three years between the time that the marriage contract with written and when the marriage was consummated. Despite this unanimity, there is still a great of disagreement among scholars on the authenticity of *ahadith* that pertain to the age of *Aisha*.

[25] It should be noted that disagreement exists on the exact date that *surah al-Qamar* was revealed as well as the age that "a young child" refers to.

> pour the water in the mouths of the people, and return to fill the water skins again and came back again to pour water in the mouths of the people.[xliv]

As you may know *Sooilfahim*, the Prophet *Muhammad* did not allow anyone younger than fifteen years of age to be present during battles. Since the Battle of *Uhud* took place in 625, this would mean that *Aisha* was at least fifteen. If this is the case, how old was *Aisha* during the second year of the *hijrah*?"

"She would have been thirteen or fourteen years old *Muntik*."

"Correct. But maybe this *hadith* has done little to convince you."[26]

"Yes *Muntik*, very little indeed!"

"Then let us move forward. We are told that all of *Abu Bakr's* children were born before the Prophet *Muhammad* received God's revelations. As we know, the Prophet *Muhammad* first received revelation in the Cave of *Hira* in 610. If we assume that *Aisha* was only one year old at this time, how old would she have been during the second year of the *hijrah*?"

"She would have been no less than thirteen years old," said *Sooilfahim*.

"Though maybe this too is a weak argument."[27]

"Very weak!" exclaimed *Sooilfahim*.

"Perhaps you will find this one more convincing. It is believed that *Aisha* was one of the earliest people to convert to Islam. The first people to convert to Islam did so in 610, as this was when the Prophet *Muhammad* first began preaching Islam. *Sooilfahim*, let us assume that *Aisha* was only five years old when she converted, how old would she be during the second year of *hijrah*?"

"This would mean she was seventeen years old."

"Let us try another approach *Sooilfahim*. It is believed that *Fatimah*, the daughter of the Prophet *Muhammad*, was five years older than *Aisha*. It is accepted that *Fatimah* was born in 606. This

---

[26] Some refute this *hadith* on grounds that the Prophet *Muhammad* gave exceptions to this rule of excluding anyone under fifteen from joining the battles.

[27] While some believe this *hadith* states that *Abu Bakr's* children were born prior to 610, others believe that the *hadith* only indicates that Abu Bakr was married before 610.

being the case, how old would this place *Aisha* during the second year of *hijrah*?"

"This would mean that Aisha was at least twelve years old."

"Correct! But perhaps you also doubt the year that *Fatimah* was born. Let us instead look at *Asma, Aisha's* eldest sister. It is reported that she died in 695 at the age of 100. This would mean she was born in 595. It is also said that she was ten years older than Aisha. Can you tell me *Sooilfahim*, how old would Aisha be during the second year of *hijrah*?"

"She would be eighteen years old."

"You see *Sooilfahim*, in all of the examples I have given you *Aisha* would be well above the age of six upon the signing of the marriage contract and more than nine at the time the marriage was consummated."

"*Muntik*, just as there are *ahadith* and historical reports supporting your claims on *Aisha's* age, there are others that support my own beliefs."

"You are correct, *Sooilfahim*. But if this is the case, why do you insist on accepting your one view?"

"I may ask the same from you! Surely you do not accuse me of choosing to believe in some *ahadith* and reject others that support my view but absolve yourself from doing the same."

"A fair accusation *Sooilfahim*. But tell me, why do you so strongly believe that Aisha was a child when she married the Prophet *Muhammad*?"

"I may ask you the same thing. The *Quran* clearly allows child marriages."

"On the contrary *Sooilfahim*. It is precisely because the *Quran* does not allow child marriages that I do not believe *Aisha* was six years of age."

"Then I am afraid you are denying clear instructions from the *Quran*. We need only to read *surah* 65, *ayah* 4 of the *Quran*:

> The waiting period of those of your women who have lost all expectation of menstruation shall be three months in case you entertain any doubt; and the same shall apply to those who have not yet menstruated. As for pregnant women, their waiting period shall be until the delivery of their burden. Allah will create ease for him who fears Allah[xlv]

Is this proof enough?"

"Not quite. If I am not mistaken, this *ayah* is in reference to getting a divorce. In Islam, there is a waiting period that must be endured before a couple may finalize their divorce.[28] Now *Sooilfahim*, according to this *ayah*, there are three types of women described. The first group refers to women whose state of menopause remains in question. The last group refers to women who are pregnant. *Sooilfahim*, who do you suppose the second group of women is?"

"Is it not obvious? The *Quran* is clearly referring to children!"

"*Sooilfahim*, if a woman must endure a waiting period, it must be because she is in the process of getting a divorce. Is this correct?"

"It is *Muntik*."

"And if a woman is in the process of getting a divorce, she must be married, do you agree?"

"Of course. There can be no other way."

"According to you, the words 'and the same shall apply to those who have not yet menstruated' in *surah* 65, *ayah* 4 refers to children. Since the waiting period only refers to married women, this must imply that it is permissible for children to be married."

"Exactly *Muntik*! Why would the *Quran* include children to endure a waiting period unless it also permitted child marriages?"

"Indeed. However I believe there is a flaw in our logic. You see, a woman is not required to endure a waiting period if she did not consummate the marriage with her husband."

"I do not see how this is related *Muntik*."

"We need only to refer to *surah* 4, *ayah* 6 to understand:

> Test the orphans until they reach the age of marriage, and then if you find them mature of mind hand over to them their property, and do not eat it up by either spending extravagantly or in haste,

---

[28] The purpose of the waiting period is two-fold. The first is to ensure that a sufficient amount of time has passed between a woman's divorce and a potential new marriage, thereby eliminating any doubt as to the identity of the father should that woman become pregnant shortly after her new marriage. The second reason is to provide a period of time where a couple may reconcile any differences they had and prevent a divorce from occurring.

> fearing that they would grow up (and claim it). If the guardian of the orphan is rich let him abstain entirely (from his ward's property); and if he is poor, let him partake of it in a fair measure. When you hand over their property to them let there be witnesses on their behalf. Allah is sufficient to take account (of your deeds).

According to this *ayah*, there are two things required of orphans before they are able to acquire their property. The first is they must reach the age of marriage, while the second condition is they must be mentally mature. Once an orphan is of age and has the capacity to manage their own affairs in a reasonable and appropriate manner, then they may inherit their property. Tell me *Sooilfahim*, what age does the *Quran* indicate is the appropriate age for marriage?"

"I am not aware of any specific age *Muntik.*"

"That is because the *Quran* never mentions an exact age. Rather, the age of marriage in this *ayah* refers to puberty. *Sooilfahim*, how can you assert that 'the same shall apply to those who have not yet menstruated' refers to children if the *Quran* requires a child to reach puberty before they are allowed to wed?"

"Then who do you propose the *Quran* is referring to if not children?"

"A great question! The *ayah* is referring to women who have either never menstruated or those who have irregular cycles. Now let us move forward *Sooilfahim*. Did the Prophet *Muhammad* have enemies?"

"Of course."

"And do you think his enemies respected him or hated him?"

"Does a man love his enemy?"

"I should think not. Tell me *Sooilfahim*, if you had an enemy would you not try to throw all that you could against him so that you may demoralize his character?"

"If he is my enemy, I do not see why I would not do worse than just that."

"Would you attempt to disparage and distort your enemies' character?"

"With all my heart."

"Should you find out something truthfully immoral about your enemy, would you not use it against him?"

"Of course! What better way to defeat my enemies' character then with the truth of his treacherous acts!"

"Then if the Prophet *Muhammad* had married *Aisha* at the age of six, why didn't any of his enemies used this marriage against him?[29]

"Perhaps they did not know," said *Sooilfahim* desperately.

"Was their marriage a secret? I should think not. Let there be no mistake, the *Quran* prohibits the marriage of a child. Marriage is a sacred union that requires mutual love and respect:

> And of His Signs is that He has created mates for you from your own kind that you may find peace in them and He has set between you love and mercy. Surely there are Signs in this for those who reflect.[xlvi]

> Believers! It is not lawful for you to become heirs to women against their will. It is not lawful that you should put constraint upon them that you may take away anything of what you have given them; (you may not put constraint upon them) unless they are guilty of brazenly immoral conduct. Live with your wives in a good manner. If you dislike them in any manner, it may be that you dislike something in which Allah has placed much good for you.[xlvii]

Marriage is not a relationship based on lust and power, but rather an equal partnership that thrives on selflessness and trust.

---

[29] When examining historical marriages, it is imperative to recognize that the norms of older societies had a lower age of consent than today. In fact, in the late 1800s the age of consent in most states in the United States was between 10 and 12 years.[IX] With respect to Medieval Europe, many children, between the ages of 5 to 10, found themselves married. Granted, such marriages were often performed for political purposes, such as to strengthen ties or to end political feuds, and were not consummated until later years. It is also worth mentioning that many prominent religious figures were also a part of this culture. For example, St. Augustine was betrothed to a 10-year-old child, while both St. Hedwig of Silesia and St. Rita of Cascia were married at the age of 12. Even in the United States today, underage marriages are not uncommon, with many states allowing children to marry so long as there is parental consent or judicial approval. In March of 2017, the Republican-led House of New Hampshire struck down a bill that would raise the minimum age of marriage to 18, effectively allowing the current age of marriage for girls to remain at 13 and boys at 14.

Muslims and the Prevalence of Terrorism

A child from the crowd yelled: "Speak to him of how Muslims are responsible for most of our troubles."

"*Muntik*, we do not charge all Muslims as being makers of mischief. However, I think you would agree that all makers of mischief are Muslims,"[30] said *Kazab*.

"On what basis do you make such a claim?" asked *Muntik*.

"Have you forgotten about the tragedy that occurred in these lands? Ten men were brought forth and found to be guilty – all were Muslims."

"An unfortunate incident. *Kazab*, do you happen to know how many people helped these ten men?"

"I do not know for they hold their tongues when asked."

"This is not surprising. How would you feel if we assumed that it was 100 Muslim men that were involved in this tragic event?"

"Quite comfortable."

"Now tell me *Kazab*, how does an ant appear in front of an elephant?"

---

[30] There are generally two accusations made regarding Islam and terrorism. The first is that while not all Muslims are terrorists, all terrorists are Muslim, as echoed by Fox host Brian Kilmeade and Finnish Member of Parliament Teuvo Hakkarainen. The second accusation is that there is a considerably large percent of the total Muslim population who are terrorists. In 2010, radio talk show host Glenn Beck stated that ten percent of all Muslims are terrorists.[III] A few years later, author and journalist Brigitte Gabriel made similar remarks, however estimates the number to be closer to 15-25% according to, in her words, "all intelligent services around the world." According to both the Institute of Economic and Peace and the United States Department of State's bureau of counterterrorism and countering violent extremist, the number of terror attacks in 2015 is estimated to be around 12,000. For the sake of simplicity, if it is assumed that 100% of terror attacks were committed by Muslims (which is certainly not the case) and that each attack was designed, planned, and executed by 100 individuals, this would imply that in 2015 there were a total of 1,200,000 Muslim terrorists. With a global population of over 1.6 billion, this would amount to 0.075% of the total Muslim population.

"Quite insignificant."

"What of a small fish in front of a great whale?"

"Why, it is nothing."

"What of a house in front of a castle?"

"A shameful sight! The house is not even worthy of comparison."

"*Kazab*, how many Muslims live across all the lands?"

"Far too many to count."

"And how do 100 Muslims stand among them? Are they not like the ant, the small fish, and the tent?"[31]

"They are," said *Kazab* reluctantly.

"I am not here to defend a people but rather a faith. As a faith, it must be judged according to its teachings and not through the actions of its followers. For as we know, a man or woman may act contrary to their faith yet still hold on to the name of their religion. I look around and see a people who would condemn a Muslim harsher than a non-Muslim though the Muslim's crime might be less severe. I

---

[31] There has been an immense amount of rhetoric focused on portraying the United States as a vulnerable state that has been plagued by Islamic terrorism. While it is certainly true that Islamic terrorism has dominated global terrorism, how susceptible has the United States been to Islamic terrorism? Do Muslim Americans truly pose a unique threat to the United States, and are Muslim terrorists the largest threat to the United States? According to a study by sociologist Charles Kurzman at the University of North Carolina, in 2016 there were a total of 46 Muslim Americans (out of a total of 3.3 million American Muslims) with links to violent extremism; of the 46, only 24 were "implicated in a concrete terrorist plot."[IV] These plots claimed a total of 54 lives, 49 of which occurred during the Pulse nightclub shooting in Orlando. According to *Terrorism 2002-2005,* a report released by the FBI that outlines all terrorist attacks directed against the United States from 1980-2005, there were almost 300 terrorist attacks against the United States.[V] During this time period, the top five terrorist groups responsible for the most deaths were the Earth Liberation Front, the Ejercito Popular Burica Macheteros, the Animal Liberation Front, the Jewish Defense League, and Omega 7. These groups carried out 104 attacks (about 33% of all terrorist attacks from 1980-2005). During this time period, terrorism by Jewish terrorist groups accounted for 7% of all attacks while Muslim terrorism accounted for 5%. Interestingly enough, the Global Terrorism Database lists just fewer than 1,000 terrorist attacks directed against the United States during this same time period. The top ten terrorist organizations, which were responsible for 70% of attacks, also included anti-abortion activists and the Army of God (a Christian terrorist organization); Islamic terrorism was not a major cause of terrorism.

look around and see a people who attribute any wrong doing of a Muslim to his religion while making no connections between a non-Muslim man's sins and his religion. If we ever hope to progress we must look pass such differences and hold all people to an equal standard."

Islam's Commandment of Killing Non-Muslims

An elder man from the crowd yelled: "Speak to him of how Islam commands the murder of non-Muslims!"

Kazab stepped forward and said in a grand voice, "*Muntik*, you wish to restore the faith in the traditions of these peoples' ancestors. A noble gesture if it were not for their forefather's hateful beliefs."

"A strong accusation indeed," said *Muntik* as his eyes met *Kazab*.

"Do you deny it? The *Quran* clearly mandates the killing of non-Muslims. Is this the type of tradition you wish to revive among these people?"

"I find this charge too outlandish to accept," said *Muntik*.

"Do you? Allow me to quote *surah* 9, *ayah* 5 of the *Quran* that commands such murderous acts:

> But when the sacred months expire slay those who associate others with Allah in His Divinity wherever you find them; seize them, and besiege them, and lie in wait for them. But if they repent and establish the Prayer and pay Zakat, leave them alone. Surely Allah is All-Forgiving, Ever-Merciful.[xlviii]

This *ayah* clearly commands the Muslims to kill indiscriminately."

"*Kazab*, what do you know of the context of this *ayah*?"

"I have provided the *ayah* in its entirety *Muntik* and have left nothing out."

"Of course. But I was speaking about the historical context that this *ayah* refers to. If it is okay with you, allow me to explain," said *Muntik*.

"Please do."

"As you may know, the Prophet *Muhammad* began preaching in private and often met with his early followers in secret. It was when he began preaching publically that the *Quraysh* began their hostile opposition to the Prophet *Muhammad* and his followers. The *Quraysh* opposed the Prophet *Muhammad* for a couple of reasons.

First, the *Quraysh* relied heavily on pilgrims visiting the *Ka'aba*, which housed 100s of Pagan idols, as a source of income. As a result, they saw the Prophet *Muhammad's* teaching of a single God and his denouncing of polytheism as a direct threat to their financial security. They also opposed the Prophet *Muhammad's* preaching on social and economic justice and equality for this would mean that the *Quraysh* were neither better nor more entitled than others. Remember, the *Quran* says:

> But no; you do not treat the orphan honourably, and do not urge one another to feed the poor, and greedily devour the entire inheritance, and love the riches, loving them ardently.[xlix]

The *Quraysh* lived at the peak of their society's social hierarchy. They were unwilling to give up their wealth, power, and authority in exchange for a life of equality among those they saw as weak and poor. Each time the Prophet *Muhammad* preached of equality and of One God, the aggression of the *Quraysh* grew.[32] Those who accepted Islam were imprisoned, beaten, starved, and tortured in horrific ways. Some of the Prophet *Muhammad's* followers were forced to flee to Abyssinia, a Christian empire, to avoid persecution. Unable to tolerate that his followers have secured a haven for themselves, the *Quraysh* dispatched an envoy to the king of Abyssinia, bringing with them gifts to both the king and his clergy in hopes of winning over their trust. The *Meccan* envoy claimed that the Muslims believed in a religion unlike that of their forefathers and even of the king himself. The king asked the Muslims about their religion and one of them replied:

---

[32] In his work, *The Encyclopedia of Middle East Wars*, Professor Spencer C. Tucker at Texas Christian University, a Fulbright scholar and ex-intelligence analyst, writes: "As *Muhammad's* group of followers grew, the leadership of *Mecca*, including *Muhammad's* own tribe, perceived them as a threat. Some of the early converts to Islam came from the disaffected and disadvantaged segments of society. Most important, the Muslims' new set of beliefs implicitly challenged the *Meccans'* and the *Quraysh* tribe's guardianship over the *Ka'aba*, the holy site dedicated to the gods and goddesses of the area, which hosted an annual pilgrimage. The city's leading merchants attempted to persuade *Muhammad* to cease his preaching, but he refused. In response, the city leadership persecuted *Muhammad's* followers, and many fled the city." [p. 849].

> O king! We were plunged in the depth of ignorance and barbarism; we adored idols, we lived in unchastity, we ate the dead bodies, and we spoke abominations, we disregarded every feeling of humanity, and the duties of hospitality and neighborhood were neglected; we knew no law but that of the strong, when Allah raised among us a man, of whose birth, truthfulness, honesty, and purity we were aware; and he called to the Oneness of Allah, and taught us not to associate anything with Him. He forbade us the worship of idols; and he enjoined us to speak the truth, to be faithful to our trusts, to be merciful and to regard the rights of the neighbours and kith and kin; he forbade us to speak evil of women, or to eat the substance of orphans; he ordered us to fly from the vices, and to abstain from evil; to offer prayers, to render alms, and to observe fast. We have believed in Him, we have accepted his teachings and his injunctions to worship Allah, and not to associate anything with Him, and we have allowed what He has allowed, and prohibited what He has prohibited. For this reason, our people have risen against us, have persecuted us in order to make us forsake the worship of Allah and return to the worship of idols and other abominations. They have tortured and injured us, until finding no safety among them, we have come to your country, and hope you will protect us from oppression.[l]

Pleased with his response, the king allowed the Muslim refugees to stay within his kingdom where they were protected and allowed to worship freely. Adamant on sabotaging the Muslims, the *Meccans* claimed that the Prophet *Muhammad's* religion blasphemies the Prophet Jesus:

> On the morrow, the two envoys again went to the king and said that Muhammad [pbuh] and his followers blasphemed Jesus Christ. Again the Muslims were summoned and asked what they thought of Jesus. Ja'far again stood up and replied: "We speak about Jesus as we have been taught by our Prophet [pbuh], that is, he is the servant of Allah, His Messenger, His spirit and His Word breathed into Virgin Mary." The king at once remarked, "Even so do we believe. Blessed be you, and blessed be your master." Then turning to the frowning envoys and to his bishops who got angry, he said: "You may fret and fume as you like but Jesus is nothing more than what Ja'far has said about him." He then assured the Muslims of full protection. He returned to the envoys of Quraysh, the gifts they had brought with them and sent them away. The Muslims lived in Abyssinia (Ethiopia) unmolested for a number of years till they returned to Medina.[li]

The Prophet *Muhammad* also endured abuse at the hands of the *Quraysh*. It was only because of his uncle, *Abu Talib*, a leader of one of the *Quraysh* clans, that the Prophet *Muhammad* had some form of protection. Though this is not to say that the Prophet *Muhammad* did not endure physical or verbal abuse. After six years of public preaching, the Prophet *Muhammad* found himself without any protection after his uncle's passing. With no other choice but to flee for his life, the Prophet *Muhammad* went to the city of *Taif*. Fearing the wrath of the *Quraysh*, the people of *Taif* rejected the Prophet *Muhammad's* message of Islam and even threw stones at him through the streets, forcing him to flee back to Mecca. A few years later, the Prophet *Muhammad* learned that the *Quraysh* had plotted to assassinate him. With no other choice, the Prophet *Muhammad* and his companions fled to *Yathrib*."

"You have bored us all to death *Muntik*. What does any of this have to do with this murderous *ayah*?"

"I ask that you give me a little more time *Kazab*. I promise I will address your point and more! Years into their stay in *Yathrib*, the Prophet *Muhammad* had a premonition that he entered the city of *Mecca* and performed a pilgrimage at the *Ka'aba*. Filled with rejoice, the Prophet *Muhammad* and 1,400 of his followers embarked on a peaceful march towards *Mecca*. Once the Muslims arrived, the *Meccans* refused to allow the pilgrims to enter! The dispute was ultimately resolved with the Treaty of *Hudaybiyyah*, which granted ten years of peace between the Prophet *Muhammad* and his allies and the *Quraysh* and their allies.[33] About two years into the agreement, the *Quraysh* had broken the treaty.[34] It was at this point that the

---

[33] The Treaty of *Hudaybiyyah* constituted more than just a peace deal. It also mandated that the Muslims forgo their pilgrimage that year and instead authorized their return the following year but for no more than three days. The treaty also stipulated that any person who escapes from *Mecca* to *Yathrib* must be returned to *Mecca*; this was presumably to prevent the Prophet *Muhammad* from gaining further support. On the other hand, if a person leaves *Yathrib* and enters *Mecca*, the *Meccans* would be under no obligation to turn them away. Lastly, the treaty allowed both the Prophet *Muhammad* and the *Quraysh* to enter into alliances with other tribes.

[34] The treaty was broken when the *Banu Bakr*, a tribe allied with the *Quraysh*, attacked and killed men of the *Banu Khuza'a*, a tribe allied with the Prophet *Muhammad*.

Prophet *Muhammad* and 10,000 of his men marched towards *Mecca* and essentially entered the city unopposed. Now *Kazab*, do you happen to know when the *ayah* you recited was revealed?"

"I do not," muttered *Kazab*."

"Come now my friend, surely you can venture a guess. Pick up where I left off!"

"Well then it must have been upon their entry into *Mecca*."

"Precisely! It was at this time that *surah* 9, *ayahs* 1-4 was revealed, when the Prophet *Muhammad* recited:

> This is a declaration of disavowal by Allah and His Messenger to those who associate others with Allah in His Divinity and with whom you have made treaties: "You may go about freely in the land, for four months, but know well that you will not be able to frustrate Allah, and that Allah will bring disgrace upon those who deny the Truth." This is a public proclamation by Allah and His Messenger to all people on the day of the Great Pilgrimage: "Allah is free from all obligation to those who associate others with Allah in His Divinity; and so is His Messenger. If you repent, it shall be for your own good; but if you turn away, then know well that you will not be able to frustrate Allah. So give glad tidings of a painful chastisement to those who disbelieve. In exception to those who associate others with Allah in His Divinity are those with whom you have made treaties and who have not violated their treaties nor have backed up anyone against you. Fulfill your treaties with them till the end of their term. Surely Allah loves the pious."[lii]

Here the *Quran* states that the people of *Mecca* will have four months, beginning from the time the Prophet *Muhammad* entered Mecca, to consider their options."

"And what options are those *Muntik*?"

"A great question! There were three options that they may choose from. The first is they may continue to wage war against the Prophet *Muhammad* and his followers. The second is they may choose to repent for their actions and convert to Islam. Lastly, the people of *Mecca* may choose to leave in peace."

"Convert to Islam? This is coming from the faith that prides itself on the belief that there is to be no compulsion in religion!"

"Do not misunderstand my words *Kazab*. These *ayahs* do not force anyone to convert. In fact, they may choose to hold onto their

Pagan faith but would then be required to leave *Mecca*," said *Muntik*.

"A peaceful religion indeed! Forcing those outside of your faith to leave the place they once called home," sneered *Kazab*.

"Do not forget that this is a unique situation, for there are a number of examples throughout history of non-Muslims being allowed to practice their faith while living under Islamic rule. Let us not forget that the people of *Mecca* are the same individuals who humiliated, harassed, tortured, and persecuted the Prophet *Muhammad* and his followers. Or do you choose to forget all of those who were murdered for no reason other than believing in equality between the rich and the poor, the strong and the weak? Despite all this, these people were given a chance to walk away in peace without being charged for their most evil of crimes. Not only that, but they were given four months before they had to make a decision!"

"You have presented a convincing case *Muntik*, but I am afraid you have rambled on for so long that you have forgotten to address the *ayah* I recited and the main issue at hand – namely the killing of non-Muslims. Allow me to recite *surah* 9, *ayah* 5 once more:

> But when the sacred months expire slay those who associate others with Allah in His Divinity wherever you find them; seize them, and besiege them, and lie in wait for them. But if they repent and establish the Prayer and pay Zakat, leave them alone. Surely Allah is All-Forgiving, Ever-Merciful.[liii]

Come now *Muntik*, what do you have to say?"

"*Kazab*, do you not recognize its meaning or are you purposely attempting to deceive us? This *ayah* only applies to those who chose the first option that we just discussed – to fight and take up arms against the Prophet *Muhammad*.[35] In fact, I trust that if we read the very next *ayah*, this may become a little clearer:

> And if any of those who associate others with Allah in His Divinity

---

[35] This *ayah* is often cited by critics of Islam as proof that the *Quran* permits the killing of non-Muslims. By presenting this *ayah* without any background, its entire historical context and the specific parameters in which it applied to is lost.

> seeks asylum, grant him asylum that he may hear the Word of Allah, and then escort him to safety for they are a people who do not know.[liv]

You see *Kazab*, even in the heat of battle if someone asks to learn more of Islam, Muslims are required to honor that request and escorted that person to safety."

"Very well *Muntik*, you may have acquitted one *ayah* but there is another *ayah* that commands the same! Just listen to *surah* 2, *ayah* 191:

> Kill them whenever you confront them and drive them out from where they drove you out. (For though killing is sinful) wrongful persecution is even worse than killing. Do not fight against them near the Holy Mosque unless they fight against you; but if they fight against you kill them, for that is the reward of such unbelievers.[lv]

Let me guess – I have not taken into consideration some historical event that would have revolutionized my understanding of this *ayah*," said *Kazab* mockingly.

"*Kazab*, why did you not recite the *ayah* before or after this one? No matter. The *ayah* immediately preceding it states:

> Fight in the way of Allah against those who fight against you but do not transgress, for Allah does not love transgressors.[lvi]

This *ayah* illustrates two important points. The first is the instruction to only fight those who instigate – in other words, fighting must be out of self-defense. Second, even when fighting out of self-defense, there are limits in place that one should adhere to so as not to transgress outside of what is appropriate.[36] In the case that a Muslim finds himself fighting out of self-defense, then they may abide by the guidance of *ayah* 191. In fact, the next case even instructs Muslims to forgive those who initiated the fighting:

---

[36] According to Islamic jurisprudence, Muslims are forbidden from killing women, children, or those unable to fight. In addition, fighters are prohibited from damaging civilian areas, including their crops, land, and livestock.

> Then if they desist, know well that Allah is Ever-Forgiving, Most Compassionate.[lvii]

You see *Kazab*, these *ayahs* only instruct Muslims to fight out of self-defense. I am sure you will be pleased to hear that one of the proceeding *ayahs* explicitly forbids Muslims from inflicting any more harm than was inflicted onto them:

> The sacred month for the sacred month; sanctities should be respected alike (by all concerned). Thus, if someone has attacked you, attack him just as he attacked you, and fear Allah and remain conscious that Allah is with those who guard against violating the bounds set by Him.[lviii]

Lastly, even in the heat of battle a Muslim must show mercy to his enemy if they cease to fight. Imagine that! Come now *Kazab*, are there any other *ayahs* within the *Quran* that you believe commands Muslims to kill non-Muslims or others indiscriminately? I will take your silence as a no. We must remember that in order to unravel the true meaning of the *Quran*, we must understand the historical context. Islam does not command the murder of any being, for the *Quran* says that the murder of a single individual equates to the murder of all mankind:

> Therefore We ordained for the Children of Israel that he who slay a soul unless it be (in punishment) for murder or for spreading mischief on earth shall be as if he had slain all mankind; and he who saves a life shall be as if he had given life to all mankind.[lix]

The *Quran* commands Muslims to attack when attacked and to show compassion when it is asked for.[37] Allow me to end with some words

---

[37] Despite Western belief, *Quranic ayah*s calling for Muslims to fight and engage in war are not synonymous with *jihad*. *Jihad* is erroneously translated from Arabic as "holy war," and is often associated with the Crusade wars. In fact, the Arabic word for holy is *muqaddas* while the Arabic word for war is *harb*. In reality, *jihad* translates to struggle, and is an Islamic concept that means to strive towards some greater good. Specifically, there are two types of *jihad* – an internal and an external. Internal *jihad* refers to any personal struggle whereas external *jihad* refers to informing others of the teachings of God and defending against those who fight against you.

from the Prophet *Muhammad*. During the Battle of *Uhud*, the Muslim army had suffered significant losses from the *Meccans*. Despite being badly injured, the Prophet *Muhammad* uttered the following words about the *Meccans*:

> It has been narrated on the authority of 'Abdullah who said: It appeared to me as if I saw the Messenger of Allah (Peace be upon him) (and heard him) relate the story of a Prophet who had been beaten by his people, was wiping the blood from his face and was saying. My Lord, forgive my people, for they do not know.[lx]

Islam teaches that compassion and mercy guide your moral compass."

The Practice of Stoning in Islam

A woman from the crowd yelled: "Speak to him of how Islam commands death by stoning!"

"*Muntik*, you have heard the charge. Tell us, what do you make of the *Quran's* commandments of stoning?" asked *Kazab*.

"How can I comment on an *ayah* that does not exist? There is not a single *ayah* in the *Quran* that calls for stoning as punishment. I assume you meant to say *ahadith*?"

"Why, yes *Muntik*."

"I thought so. As you know, the Arabic word for stoning is *rajm* and this is never used in the *Quran* as a prescription for punishment. In fact, the only time the word *rajm* is used is when disbelievers against the Prophet *Muhammad* uttered it:

> The people of the town said: "We believe you are an evil omen for us. If you do not desist, we will stone you or you will receive a grievous chastisement from us."[lxi]

Tell me *Kazab*, in your view when does Islam prescribe the punishment of stoning?"

"Is it not obvious? Islam clearly mandates that those who commit *zina*[38] and for those who commit apostasy."

"How interesting! I shall deal with this issue of apostasy first as it is the least complicated of the two."

"I think you will find it more difficult to deal with these accusations than you think *Muntik*, but by all means proceed."

"*Kazab*, are you familiar with *surah* 2, *ayah* 256?"

"I am," muttered *Kazab*.

"Allow me to remind our audience:

---

[38] In Arabic, the word *zina* refers to any unlawful sexual intercourse. Therefore, fornication and adultery would both fall into the category of *zina*.

> There is no compulsion in religion.[lxii]

How can you claim that the *Quran* mandates a punishment for apostasy, by stoning to death no less, when the *Quran* clearly states that there is no compulsion in religion?"

"The *ahadith* are clear on this matter *Muntik*."

"But is the *Quran* not more clear?

> And proclaim: "This is the Truth from your Lord. Now let him who will, believe; and let him who will, disbelieve.[lxiii]
>
> Had your Lord so willed, all those who are on the earth would have believed. Will you, then, force people into believing?[lxiv]

Surely you do not put more faith in the *ahadith* then the *Quran*?"

"Do you deny that there are those who are put to death for leaving Islam?"

"*Kazab*, are we to judge a faith on its teachings or its observer's practices? Surely the mother who starves her children and leaves them uncovered in the cold does not represent the dignity and blessings of motherhood. In the same way, it is the teachings of Islam that come to define the faith and not necessarily the way it is practiced, for as you know, we as humans are imperfect and prone to grave errors."

"Enough already, you have made your point. Tell me then what of *zina*, or will you deny that the *Quran* views this as a punishable offense?"

"I shall make no such denial *Kazab*. The *Quran* does indeed prescribe a punishment for *zina*:

> Those who [commit zina] - whether female or male - flog each one of them with a hundred lashes. And let not tenderness for them deter you from what pertains to Allah's religion, if you do truly believe in Allah and the Last Day; and let a party of believers witness their punishment.[lxv]

The punishment for *zina* is 100 lashes."

"*Muntik*, do you knowingly change the words of the *Quran* or is it out of ignorance?"

"I am afraid it must be out of ignorance for I do not intend to misguide you."

"The *ayah* you have recited is referring specifically to fornication – not adultery."

"An interesting opinion *Kazab*."

"It is more than an opinion *Muntik*, it is a fact."

"Then allow us to arrive at this truth together. As you know, the Arabic word *zina* refers to any unlawful intimacy including both fornication and adultery. It surprises me to hear you say that this *ayah* only refers to fornication. What do you imagine is the punishment for adultery *Kazab*?"

"Is it not obvious. Islam clearly mandates stoning as the punishment for adultery. There are many *ahadith* that clearly prescribe death by stoning as punishment for adultery. The fact that both the *Quran* and the *ahadith* prescribe different punishments can only mean that the *Quran* is referring to fornication while the *ahadith* are referring to adultery, for just as adultery is a more severe offense than fornication, stoning is a more severe punishment than lashes."

"If this is the case, help me make sense of the following *ayah*:

> And those of you who cannot afford to marry free, believing women (muhsanat), then marry such believing women whom your right hands possess. Allah knows all about your faith. All of you belong to one another. Marry them, then, with the leave of their guardians, and give them their bridal-due in a fair manner that they may live in the protection of wedlock rather than be either mere objects of unfettered lust or given to secret love affairs. Then if they become guilty of immoral conduct after they have entered into wedlock, they shall be liable to half the penalty to which free women (muhsanat) are liable.[lxvi]

This *ayah* states that the punishment for women whom your right hand possess that commit adultery is half of that imposed on free women. Enlighten us *Kazab*, how would you impose half of the death penalty through stoning?"

"I do not know."

"And half the punishment of 100 lashes?"

"It would be fifty lashes," said *Kazab* begrudgingly.

"Correct! It is clear *Kazab* that the punishment for *zina* in Islam, whether for fornication or adultery, is 100 lashes."

"And what does any of this matter *Muntik*? I am sure many would rather be put to death than to stand under the scorching sun and be whipped like some animal."

"Then allow me to put things in perspective. What conditions must be met in order for someone to be punished for *zina*?"

"The *Quran* says there must be four witnesses,"[39] replied *Kazab*.

"Correct! And are these just any four witnesses?"

"I do not understand."

"While you are right that four witnesses are required to testify that *zina* has occurred, there are specific criteria that must be met. Allow me to explain. First, four individuals must witness the act of *zina*. Second, these witnesses must be pious and of the highest moral standing without a blemish in their religious character. Third, they must all be present at the time of testimony. Lastly, their testimony must be identical. Perhaps you are familiar with *Pericope Adulterae*, or the passage of adultery in the Bible?"

"I am *Muntik*."

"Excellent. Then as you are already aware, a group of people brought a woman who had committed adultery to the Prophet Jesus and asked if she should be stoned according to the laws set forth by the Prophet Moses. When pressed further, the Prophet Jesus simply replied:

> "Let any one of you who is without sin be the first to throw a stone at her."[lxvii]

Eventually the group dispersed, for who among us is without sin? It is this level of piety that is required when testifying against someone for committing *zina*. In fact *Kazab*, in the event that even one of the four witnesses fails to be present at the time of testimony, or if all

---

[39] In *surah* 4, *ayah* 15 the *Quran* states there must be four witnesses to testify that *zina* had occurred. This *ayah* also prescribes a punishment for *zina*, but was later abrogated and replaced with the punishment of whipping as written in *surah* 24, *ayah* 2.

four accounts are not identical, then these witnesses will bear punishment for falsely accusing someone of *zina*:

> Those who accuse honourable women (of unchastity) but do not produce four witnesses, flog them with eighty lashes, and do not admit their testimony ever after. They are indeed transgressors, except those of them that repent thereafter and mend their behaviour. For surely Allah is Most Forgiving, Ever Compassionate.[lxviii, 40]

It is only after all of these conditions are met that someone may be punished for *zina*.[41, 42] Despite all that we have discussed *Kazab*, I want you to remember that in Islam the door for repentance is always open. In fact, the Prophet *Muhammad* forgave many for their crimes without punishment as they had repented:

> Unless he repents and believes and does righteous works. For such, Allah will change their evil deeds into good deeds. Allah is Ever Forgiving, Most Compassionate.[lxix]

Do not underestimate the forgiveness of God."

---

[40] Some critics of Islam assert that the *Quranic* requirement of four witnesses applies to rape. This is entirely untrue. It would be inconceivable to allow bystanders to witness a rape in order for the rapist to be accused of a crime. There is a popular *hadith* where the Prophet *Muhammad* said: "When people see a wrong-doer and do nothing to stop him, they may well be visited by God with a punishment."

[41] Interestingly enough, some scholars regard the punishment of stoning as only a theoretical one. In other words, while they regard the *ahadith* that prescribe stoning as authentic, the criteria required to impose the punishment is virtually impossible to meet. The purpose of this unenforceable punishment is to emphasize the wrongdoing of *zina* and to dissuade people from even contemplating such an offense.

[42] In the event that a person is to be punished, there are specific criteria describing how the punishment should take place. First, the whipping cannot take place on a hot day or a cold day. Second, the person imposing the punishment cannot raise their arm above their head in order to prevent unnecessary harm; only moderate force should be used. In addition, the face and any sensitive areas must be avoided.

Virgins in Heaven

A woman from the crowd yelled: "Speak to him of Islam's perverted view of heaven!"

"*Muntik*, tell us what you think of Islam's promise that a man will receive seventy-two virgins in heaven?"[43] asked *Kazab*.

"I know of no such promise!"

"Do not deny what exists. There is a *hadith* that gives supports to this idea of virgins in heaven:

> "The least of the people of Paradise in position is the one with eighty thousand servants and seventy-two wives. He shall have a tent of pearl, peridot, and corundum set up for him."[lxx]

Are these words not clear?"

"Tell me, on what basis do you trust in this *hadith*'s legitimacy?" asked *Muntik*.

"I have no reason to believe otherwise," scuffed *Kazab*.

"Come, then let us examine this *hadith* together. First I must ask you, is there any mentioning of seventy-two virgins in heaven within the *Quran*?"

"There is not," replied *Kazab*.

"I did not think so. I also am not aware of any significance that the number seventy-two has. Do you?"

"No *Muntik*, I too am unaware."

"No matter! Let us then examine this *hadith* together. This *hadith* mentions that in heaven, we will receive three things: 80,000 servants, seventy-two wives, and an abundance of wealth. Though we mustn't forget that this *hadith* also states that for some, these

---

[43] It is interesting to note that while this notion of receiving seventy-two virgins in heaven is quite common in the West, this "Islamic belief" has little audience in the Islamic world.

rewards will be even greater. *Kazab*, if I granted you only one wish, what would you ask for?"

"I do not see what this has to do with anything, though I suppose I would ask for immortality."

"And if I offered you another wish?"

"Eternal youth."

"And another?"

"To dine with the finest food and wine."

"What else?"

"Why, how grand life would be with a woman by my side!"

"Anything else?"

"What else could I want *Muntik*? I have everything I could ever need!" exclaimed *Kazab*.

"In heaven, you are immortal, eternally youthful, you dine with the finest of food and drink, and you have a companion by your side. It seems that just by being in heaven, you have everything you could ever want. *Kazab*, if you could not think of more than four wants or desires, then what purpose is there for 80,000 servants? Better yet, why not have a single servant who could accomplish what 80,000 cannot? But even this notion of servitude in heaven is problematic. As described by the *Quran*, heaven is a place where all of the heart's desires are fulfilled. If this is the case, what purpose would even a single servant fulfill if you could have whatever your heart desired?"

"I do not know," muttered *Kazab*.

"Nor do I."

"*Muntik*, you cannot deny that the *Quran* mentions these virgins."

"I do not deny that such creations will exist in heaven. As you said, the *Quran* mentions *houris* in several *ayahs*:

> Verily the God-fearing shall be in a secure place amidst gardens and springs. Attired in silk and brocade, they shall be arrayed face to face. Thus shall it be: and We shall espouse them to fair, wide-eyed maidens. While resting in security, they shall call for all kinds of fruit.[lxxi]

> The God-fearing shall be reclining on couches facing each other, and We shall wed them to maidens with large, beautiful eyes.[lxxii]

Kazab, what exactly is a *houri*?"

"You know as well as I do that it is a female virgin made as companions for men in heaven."

"Perhaps, but how would you translate the word *houris* from Arabic?

"I do not know *Muntik*."

"Then allow me to help you. As you might expect, though similar, there are a number of ways *houris* can be translated. Some translate them as 'gazelle-eyed' or 'pure companions of beautiful eyes.' In fact, the *Quranic ayahs* that we have just mentioned refers to them as 'wide-eyed maidens' or 'maidens with large, beautiful eyes.' When the *Quran* describes *houris*, it refers to them as youthful,[44] modest,[45] and even compares their beauty to that of pearls.[46] Why is it then that you only refer to them as virgins?"

"Do you deny that this is one of their attributes?"

"I do not *Kazab*, but it troubles me that this is where your emphasis lies, for as I have demonstrated this is not how they are portrayed in the *Quran*. This attribution of virginity is only one of their many qualities and is meant merely to symbolize their purity.[47] Let us now look at what the *Quran* tells us about heaven:

> The Ever-lasting Gardens which they shall enter and so shall the righteous from among their fathers, and their spouses, and their offspring. And angels shall enter unto them from every gate, and say: 'Peace be upon you. You merit this reward for your steadfastness.' How excellent is the ultimate abode![lxxiii]

> (On the other hand), Allah will cause those who believed and acted righteously to enter the Gardens beneath which rivers flow. They shall be decked in them with bracelets of gold and pearls and their raiment shall be of silk.[lxxiv]

---

[44] *Surah* 78, *ayah* 33

[45] *Surah* 37, *ayah* 48

[46] *Surah* 56, *ayah* 23

[47] While it is generally believed that *houris* refer to companions of perfect beauty, there still remains a great deal of obscurity over its exact meaning. In fact, some scholars believe *houris* can either be male or female and thus will be united with both spouseless men and women.

> Allah has promised the believing men and believing women Gardens beneath which rivers flow. They shall abide in it. There are delightful dwelling places for them in the Gardens of Eternity. They shall, above all, enjoy the good pleasure of Allah. That is the great achievement.[lxxv]

> And those Foremost, they will be the foremost! They shall be near-stationed (to their Lord), in the Gardens of Bliss.[lxxvi]

> Enter Paradise joyfully, both you and your spouses.[lxxvii]

Heaven is an abode where you may have whatever your heart desires."

"All I have heard is that heaven is about one's physical and materialistic desires."

"Do not confuse the *Quran's* descriptions of physical excellence with the true ultimate pleasure of heaven."[48]

"And what would that be *Muntik*?"

"It is one's relationship with God:

> Allah has promised the believing men and believing women Gardens beneath which rivers flow. They shall abide in it. There are delightful dwelling places for them in the Gardens of Eternity. They shall, above all, enjoy the good pleasure of Allah. That is the great achievement.[lxxviii]

This is the ultimate pleasure of heaven."

---

[48] Given the *Quran's* description of heaven as a dwelling of perfect beauty and filled with unworldly fruit, where men and women are adorned with silk and gold, some wonder why heaven is presented in such a materialistic fashion. The general consensus among scholars is that the pleasures of heaven are so great, that they cannot be described in words. Put another way, our minds are unable to grasp the reality of heaven. Therefore, heaven is described in the only way that we are able to understand it. *Ibn Sina*, regarded as one of the greatest minds and philosophers in Islamic history, believed that the highest form of pleasure one can attain in heaven is one of mental and spiritual intellect, whereas physical descriptions of gardens and gold were lesser pleasures. Though many viewed *Ibn Sina's* philosophy on heaven as controversial, the *Quran* does state that the greatest pleasure of heaven is not physical but rather one's relationship with God.

Islam on Slavery and its Reformation

A man from the crowd yelled: "Speak to him of Islam's support for slavery!"

"*Muntik*, does Islam believe all humans are equal?" asked *Kazab*.

"In the eyes of God we are all equal," replied *Muntik*.

"Is God All-Good?"

"Of course."

"All-Loving?"

"Yes."

"All-Merciful?"

"Surely."

"Then tell us why didn't God abolish slavery under Islam? How can Islam be a religion of equality when it allowed slavery? How can Islam accept a hierarchical system that is defined by a superior owning an inferior, yet still claim that God loves all His children and that all men are equal?"

"Rest easy *Kazab* for I believe I can reconcile this matter if you will only give me some time."

"Then proceed *Muntik*."

"In order for us to truly understand the issue of slavery within Islamic doctrine, we must first understand it within the context of pre-Islamic Arabia. Once we have accomplished this, I am sure you will come to accept that while Islam allowed slavery, the way in which it was institutionalized under Islam actually led to its abolishment."

"A hopeful statement, *Muntik* but I am a man who requires more than empty words."

"Tell me *Kazab*, what value does a slave have?"

"Is the answer not obvious? A slave is a human without worth. Their lives are filled with nothing but hardship, labor, and torment."

"And much worse we can assume!"

"Much worse *Muntik*. A slave is like the man who must find his way through a dark maze, and when a glimpse of light is finally within reach, he falls back into the abyss."

"An awful sight indeed! Unfortunately history has done little to mend the sorrow in our hearts for many great men have condemned man into a life of servitude.[49, 50] Even some of the world's great religions speak words on slavery that may make our minds uneasy. Exodus 21:20-21 and Deuteronomy 20:10-14 state:

> Anyone who beats their male or female slave with a rod must be punished if the slave dies as a direct result, but they are not to be punished if the slave recovers after a day or two, since the slave is their property.[lxxix]
>
> When you march up to attack a city, make its people an offer of peace. If they accept and open their gates, all the people in it shall be subject to forced labor and shall work for you. If they refuse to make peace and they engage you in battle, lay siege to that city. When the Lord your God delivers it into your hand, put to the sword all the men in it. As for the women, the children, the livestock and everything else in the city, you may take these as plunder for yourselves. And you may use the plunder the Lord your God gives you from your enemies.[lxxx]

Though I am sure we have barely scratched the surface of the life of a slave."

"*Muntik*, are we to spend our entire time standing here discussing the life of a slave?"

"Certainly not *Kazab*. Answer me this, does the *Quran* ever promote the practice of slavery?"

"The *Quran* may not promote its practice, but I can assure you there is not a single *ayah* in the *Quran* that forbids its practice."

---

[49] Plato believed that slaves were unworthy of freedom because they have proven themselves to be inferior. In other words, free men are free because they have shown that they are better, more powerful, and superior than their counterparts. Aristotle attempted at rationalizing this superiority-inferiority complex by asserting that "some men are born to rule, others are born to serve."

[50] Well over 1000 years after the rise of Islam, the US would find itself imposing the three-fifths cause of 1787 stating that a slave's value is equivalent to three-fifths that of a free man.

"Correct *Kazab*, but allow me to explain why this is."

"Go on, *Muntik*."

"Before the rise of Islam in the Arabian Peninsula, the idea of a slave having any value was nonexistent. They were regarded as objects – sold as ordinary possessions, sometimes along with the land they tilled. Slaves had no rights and were without freedom. Their sole purpose was to serve."

"Then why didn't Islam just forbid this practice?"

"Patience my friend! Now tell us – do you deny that the Prophet *Muhammad* reformed many facets of Pre-Islamic Arabia?"

"I fail to see what this has to do with anything, though I will indulge you for a little while longer and answer no."

"Would you agree that one area of reformation regarded idolatry?"

"Seeing as how *Mecca* went from being a Pagan society to an Islamic one, I would agree."

"As I'm sure you know, the *Quran* was not shy in speaking out against idolatry. In fact it was quite clear on its position of idol worshipping:

> Surely Allah does not forgive that a partner be ascribed to Him, although He forgives any other sins for whomever He wills. He who associates anyone with Allah in His divinity has indeed forged a mighty lie and committed an awesome sin.[lxxxi]

> (Tell them clearly that) it was revealed to you and to all Prophets before you: 'If you associate any others with Allah in His Divinity, your works will surely come to naught and you will certainly be among the losers.'[lxxxii]

These *ayahs* clearly illustrate Islam's views against idolatry."

"Oh *Muntik*, you have cut off your very legs! You have presented a grand case of the *Quran's* explicit condemnation of idolatry. Why does the *Quran* explicitly condemn Paganism yet not do the same for slavery?"

"The reason why the *Quran* directly condemned Paganism was because it is against the very core of Islam and the Abrahamic religions. It would be inconceivable for a religion whose very identity is the belief in a single God to not condemn anything that contradicts this basic principle. However this doesn't entirely answer your question as to why the *Quran* could not do the same for slavery. You see *Kazab*, slavery was deeply embedded in the economic policies of Arabia. It was so ingrained in Pre-Islamic Arabia that it was inconceivable that anyone would have embraced Islam during its infant years if it had made any direct exclamations against slavery. Perhaps of more importance was even if Islam had been successful in swiftly eliminating slavery, what would become of the newly freed slaves? How were they to integrate themselves into society? The only practical method to not only abolish the institutionalization of slavery but to also reintegrate slaves into society as free men and women was through reformation."[51]

"And exactly what reformations were made?" asked *Kazab*.

"A most excellent question! There are four areas that Islam took to reform slavery. The first was in how Islam defined righteousness:

> Righteousness does not consist in turning your faces towards the east or towards the west; true righteousness consists in believing in Allah and the Last Day, the angels, the Book and the Prophets, and in giving away one's property in love of Him to one's kinsmen, the orphans, the poor and the wayfarer, and to those who ask for help, and in freeing the necks of slaves, and in establishing Prayer and dispensing the Zakat.[lxxxiii]

---

[51] In an essay written by teacher Adam Weston, he writes: "The existence of slavery is an ancient condition. It existed long before the Qur'an was revealed to *Muhammad*, starting in 610 C.E. What is interesting is comparing the depiction of slavery in the Qur'an to the Old and New Testament. In these older Jewish and Christian holy texts, a *specific* plan to eliminate the human bondage of our temporal present is never discussed. The Qur'an, on the other hand, not only recognized the immorality of slavery in seventh century Arabia, but also sought to end it. The plan to do so is both implicit and explicit. To recognize this is to respect the Islamic attempt, in the name of Allah, to destroy an evil custom nearly thirteen centuries before America would legally and politically do the same…It recognizes that a negative institution that is deeply part of Arabic culture could not be eliminated instantly, with a single surah: 'Slavery was widely prevalent in Arabia at the time of the advent of Islam, and the Arab economy was based on it' (Hassan 374). Instead, repetition of thoughts is often used that either collectively make God's plan apparent, or build from criticism to condemnation."

This *ayah* from the *Quran* redefines righteousness to mean much more than a Muslim who simply observes his religious obligations to God in prayer. True righteousness includes the person who frees slaves."

"One *ayah* is hardly considered an effort," muttered *Kazab*.

"Then allow me to continue. Another area of reformation dealt with the act of repentance. The Prophet *Muhammad* stated that penance for a sin should come in the form of either fasting or the freeing of a slave. So, if you commit a sin, you could…?"

"Free a slave," answered *Kazab* reluctantly.

"If you missed a fast, you could…?"

"Free a slave."

"If you unintentionally inflicted harm upon another, you could…?"

"Free a slave."

"If you broke a promise to someone, you could…?"

"Free a slave."

"Correct! Let us continue. The third way in which Islam reformed slavery came in the form of *zakat*. *Surah* 9, *ayah* 60 states:

> The alms are meant only for the poor and the needy and for those who are in charge thereof, those whose hearts are to be reconciled, and to free those in bondage, and to help those burdened with debt, and for expenditure in the way of Allah, and for the wayfarer. This is an obligation from Allah. Allah is All-Knowing, All-Wise.[lxxxiv]

The riches of *zakat* were to be used for a number of reasons, which ranged from reducing state poverty to helping an individual on a journey. As described in this *ayah*, the *Quran* also instructs that from the *zakat* treasury, a part of the budget should go towards the emancipation of slaves. This treasury helped slaves in two ways. First, it provided a slave with payment for ransom money. Second, the Islamic government used the treasury in order to pay the price of a slave's freedom. Moving on, the fourth area of reformation dealt with marriage, where the *Quran* empowered and encouraged slaves to get married. *Surah* 24, *ayah* 32 states:

> Marry those of you that are single, (whether men or women), and those of your male and female slaves that are righteous. If they are

poor, Allah will enrich them out of His Bounty. Allah is Immensely Resourceful, All-Knowing.

Are you deep in thought *Kazab*, or do you hold your tongue for some other reason?" asked *Muntik*.

"I shall speak my thoughts when I am ready," said *Kazab* with hesitance.

"Then I shall continue until you are ready for I have much more to say. You see, Islam took its most drastic step in reforming slavery through the use of language. Tell me *Kazab*, what is the Arabic word for slave?"

"*Abd*."

"Precisely. And what sort of meaning did this word carry? Was it one of respect or shame?"

"It was one of shame, for what value is there in the life of a slave?" replied *Kazab*.

"Correct, however, the word *abd* later became a blessing. Islam teaches that all Muslims are slaves. All Muslims are *abeed* in that all Muslims are *abd'Allah*. The highest level of spirituality one can attain in Islam is that of servitude to God. To be called a slave of God is the ultimate blessing. Grant me if you will some time to share a story. Perhaps the best-known slave in Islamic history is *Bilal* – a Black man who was kidnapped as a young child and sold into slavery. His master belonged to the *Quraysh*, one of the most powerful tribes in *Mecca* – the same tribe that the Prophet *Muhammad* belonged to. As a slave, *Bilal* was not able to get married, own money, or bring his master to court for any injustices that occurred. One day as *Bilal* and other slaves gathered together, one of the slaves mentioned the Prophet *Muhammad*, whom the entire city knew for his honesty and generosity. The slaves began repeating the Prophet *Muhammad's* teachings of human equality and how the good will be rewarded and the wicked punished. Attracted to these teachings, *Bilal* began visiting the Prophet *Muhammad's* house to hear him preach. Shortly thereafter, *Bilal*'s master discovered these secret attendances. Furious, the master tortured *Bilal* and demanded that he denounce his belief in God and to instead worship the Pagan idols. Upon his refusal to do so, *Bilal* was ceaselessly beaten and punished. At one point, *Bilal* was laid down on the ground and had a large stone placed upon his chest as the sun beat down on him. During mid-day, *Bilal's* master came back and asked him for a response. *Bilal* simply replied 'One [God]. One [God].' *Abu Bakr*, one of the earliest companions of the Prophet *Muhammad* saw this sight and could not help but intervene. Unfortunately, his options were limited. He could not demand the master to stop for no court of justice would punish a master for mistreatment of his own slave. Instead, *Abu Bakr* paid the master a large sum of money and bought *Bilal* and freed him immediately."

"And what is so special about *Bilal*?" asked *Kazab*.

"*Bilal*'s role in Islam is more than just as an emancipated slave. Around 623 CE, the Prophet *Muhammad* chose *Bilal* from among all of the Muslims to be the first to sound the call to prayer and from that moment on, *Bilal* became the official caller to prayer. Even in 630 CE, when the Prophet *Muhammad* and his companions captured *Mecca*, *Bilal* climbed atop the *Ka'aba* and began the call to prayer. Imagine *Kazab*, a former slave standing with his feet on top of the house of God! What a glorious message. Let us not forget that the slaves who heard the Prophet *Muhammad's* message embraced Islam.[52] The Prophet *Muhammad* taught that there were two ways of interacting with slaves. The first is a requirement that they be treated with respect and dignity, while the second is advocating to free them. For those of who you are unconvinced, let me end with some words of the Prophet *Muhammad*:

> Abu Mas'ud al-Ansari reported: "When I was beating my servant, I heard a voice behind me (saying): Abu Mas'ud, bear in mind Allah

---

[52] An interesting story is that of *Zayd ibn Harithah*. As a boy, *Zayd* was captured and sold into slavery and eventually became the slave of the Prophet *Muhammad* before he had received revelations from God. After many years have passed, members of *Zayd's* tribe travelled to *Mecca* on a pilgrimage and recognized him. As the travellers hurried back home, *Zayd's* family were notified of his location and set out to meet him. When the arrived, *Zayd* told his family that he wished to remain with the Prophet *Muhammad*, at which point the Prophet *Muhammad* adopted *Zayd* as his son. Later on, *Zayd* would marry a cousin of the Prophet *Muhammad*. The significance of this story is twofold. First, it signifies how well slaves were treated under Islamic law. Second, the marriage between *Zayd* and the Prophet *Muhammad*'s cousin breaks the barrier that is traditionally built between members of distinctly different hierarchical classes.

has more dominance over you than you have upon him. I turned and (found him) to be Allah's Messenger (may peace be upon him). I said: Allah's Messenger, I set him free for the sake of Allah. Thereupon he said: Had you not done that, (the gates of) Hell would have opened for you, or the fire would have burnt you. [lxxxv]

I heard Allaah's Messenger (way sallAllaahu alayhi wa sallam) say: He who slaps his slave or beats him, the expiation for it is that he should set him free.[lxxxvi]

And he also narrated: The Prophet (saw) said: None of you must say: "My slave" (abdi) and "My slave-woman" (amati), and a slave must not say: "My lord" (rabbi or rabbati). The master (of a slave) should say: "My young man" (fataya) and "My young woman" (fatati), and a slave should say "My master" (sayyidi) and "My mistress" (sayyidati), for you are all (Allah`s) slave and the Lord is Allah, Most High. [lxxxvii, 53]

All mankind is from Adam and Eve, an Arab has no superiority over a non-Arab nor a non-Arab has any superiority over an Arab; also a white has no superiority over a black nor a black has any superiority over white except by piety and good action. Learn that every Muslim is a brother to every Muslim and that the Muslims constitute one brotherhood. Nothing shall be legitimate to a Muslim which belongs to a fellow Muslim unless it was given freely and willingly. Do not, therefore, do injustice to yourselves.[54]

My friends, the goal of Islam was not to simply extinguish the institutionalization of slavery but to abolish all of the cruelty that came with it. In the end, all Muslims are slaves of God."

---

[53] The significance of this *hadith* is it shows the extent that the Prophet *Muhammad* took in changing the language that existed among slaves and their owners. By urging slaves not to refer to their owners as lords, and owners to their slaves as slaves, it helped to break down the hierarchical barriers that existed between the two social groups.

[54] These words were from the Prophet *Muhammad's* last sermon the year that he passed.

Silence

They *Motheyeen* were dumbfounded. Never had they expected to be outwitted, in front of the entire town by a stranger, no less. For every argument they had *Muntik* had two, and every rebuttal they threw *Muntik* met straight on and brought down just as easily as it was thrown. Having exhausted all of their attacks, the *Motheyeen* were defenseless.

The piercing eyes of those in the town square began incarcerating the three-cloaked men. What were they to do? Their logic had been shattered and their lies exposed. Their rhetoric had failed and as a result the *Motheyeen* had suffered the first blow to their grip over the people. As the peoples' voices grew louder in protest of their falling leadership, the *Motheyeen* were desperate to regain control over them.

After years of abandonment, the faith of the peoples' ancestors was alive once again – and now, nothing could destroy that. With no other option, the *Motheyeen* too began embracing the faith of the past. But it was a dark embrace, one filled with perversion and falsehood.

Part Three – The Fall

Is Celebrating Christmas Permissible?

A woman from the crowd yelled: "*Muntik*, what do you think of Christmas?"[55]

"Do not ask of him what we have already taught you! Christmas is forbidden and no Muslim should ever celebrate this holiday!" exclaimed *Sakheef*.

"Tell me *Sakheef*, on what basis is the celebration of Christmas forbidden?" asked *Muntik*.

"Not only does Christmas have Pagan roots[56] but it also celebrates the birth of the Prophet Jesus. Perhaps you have forgotten

---

[55] Before evaluating Islam's perspective on celebrating Christmas, it is important to understand the holiday's origin. Was Jesus really born on December 25th? While there is no unanimity on the day that Jesus was born, most scholars do not regard December 25th to accurately represent his birth date. While the Bible offers clues, it does not mention any specific date or a time of year that Jesus was born. A common Biblical verse cited as evidence against a December birth is found in the Gospel of Luke 2:7-8, which describes shepherds watching over their herds at night at the time of Jesus' birth. Since a typical December night in Judea would be cold and rainy, scholars suggest that it would be unlikely that shepherds would be out with their flock at this time. Therefore, some believe that this verse implies that Jesus was born during the spring; however, one should be cautious in deriving information from a passage whose emphasis is more theological than it is calendric. The earliest discussion of Jesus' birthday actually comes from Clement of Alexandria, a Christian theologian who was once considered a saint by the Roman Catholic Church, who dates Jesus is birth to January 6th; interestingly enough, to this day Orthodox Armenians celebrate Christmas on January 6th. It was not until the fourth century that December 25th came to officially represent Jesus' birth and therefore Christmas.

[56] It is not uncommon to hear the claim that Christmas has Pagan origins. What significance did December 25th have in Paganism? In the Northern Hemisphere, the winter solstice marks the time of the year when daylight is the shortest. A few days later, more specifically December 25th, the lengthening in daylight becomes noticeable. Some believe that it was this observation that caused the Pagans to celebrate December 25th as the rebirth of the sun. Some argue that the decision to celebrate Christmas on December 25th was an attempt to popularize Christianity over the Pagan celebrations on a day that held significant meaning within Roman

that Islam rejects Paganism and it certainly does not believe that this day marks the Prophet Jesus' birthday."

"You are correct in your claims *Sakheef*," said *Muntik*.

"I thought you would see it my way."

"Yet I must disagree with your conclusion. What is Pagan about Christmas, is it the tree?"

"Correct."

"What about the gifts?"

"Them as well."

"And the date of December 25th?"

"The same answer as before."

"It appears that there may be quite a few Pagan traditions in Christmas."

"This is what I have been trying to tell you *Muntik*! We should do all we can to dissociate ourselves from such customs."

"Does it matter *Sakheef*?"

"Surely you are not insisting that Islam approves of Paganism?"

"Far from it! You see we have come to the conclusion that Christmas may have adopted some Pagan customs. Yet considering Christmas today does not symbolize Pagan beliefs, what does its origin matter if its present symbolism has nothing to do with Paganism? Tell me, are Christians Pagans?"

"What a foolish question *Muntik*. How can a Christian be a Pagan when one worships an idol and the other does not?"

---

society. It was not until 350 CE, when Christmas began gaining momentum within the Roman Empire, that Pope Julius I declared that December 25th would be celebrated as the birth of Jesus. Despite this official establishment, the "Christianness" of Christmas has not been without question. In fact, in the 17th century New England Puritans decided to ban Christmas, as they saw no scriptural justification for its celebration; they also wished to distance themselves from its association with Paganism. According to Scottish theologian Alexander Hislop's work, *The Two Babylons*: "The Christmas tree, now so common among us, was equally common in Pagan Rome and Pagan Egypt. In Egypt that tree was the palm-tree; in Rome it was the fir; the palm tree denoting the Pagan messiah, as Baal-Tamar, the fir referring to him as Baal-Berith." Regardless of any possible ties Christmas may have with ancient Pagan customs or whether or not December 25th actually marks Jesus is real birth, Christianity views this day as a means to commemorate and celebrate God's love for mankind as demonstrated by the sacrifice of His only Son.

"Is Christianity alike to Paganism?"

"Have you lost your mind? The two religions mix like water and oil."

"Then surely you would agree that the core values of Christianity are different than that of Paganism?"

"How could I not agree?"

"Then tell me *Sakheef*, why would our Christian brothers and sisters celebrate a holiday that symbolizes Paganism?"

"I suppose they would not."

"Even if Christmas consisted of Pagan traditions, it does not matter. To many, Christmas has come to symbolize the birth of the Prophet Jesus and God's sacrifice for man's sins."

"You have made your point *Muntik*. But no matter, Islam still refutes the belief that the Prophet Jesus was born on this date and it certainly does not believe in his sacrifice. To celebrate Christmas is to submit to the idea that the Prophet Jesus is the Son of God."

"Tell me *Sakheef*, after all that we have discussed would you agree that the symbolism and value of a holiday depends on what we associate it with? In other words, is it our personal perceptions and the beliefs that we associate those objects or holidays with that determines how we identify with them? For example, would a Christian cease to associate Christmas with the birth and sacrifice of the Prophet Jesus merely because Islam rejects the notion of a holy sacrifice?"

"Of course not. A Christian would continue to celebrate Christmas as a day symbolizing the holy birth and sacrifice."

"And would you fault the Christian for this persistence in belief?"

"How could I? If this is what they believe, how does my personal belief change how they identify with Christmas?"

"If a Muslim's perception of Christmas does not affect how a Christian views Christmas, then why is the opposite true?"

"I am afraid I do not understand what you mean *Muntik*."

"We have just agreed that regardless of what Muslims believe, it is ultimately up to Christians to determine how they identify with Christmas."

"This is indeed what we have agreed on."

"Then I ask you, if a Muslim does not believe that December 25th symbolizes the Prophet Jesus is birthday or that of the holy sacrifice, what does it matter if Christians believe the opposite? Just as your personal opinion does not change a Christian's perception of what Christmas symbolizes, a Christian's personal opinion does not change your perception of what Christmas does not symbolize. Or do you disagree?"

"No *Muntik*, your judgment is sound."

"It appears there is nothing wrong with Muslims celebrating Christmas so long as a Muslim does not identify with the Christian beliefs that contradict those of Islam."

"And what exactly would Muslims gain from celebrating a holiday that they do not have any religious ties to?"

"No religious ties *Sakheef*? Remember that to be a Muslim is to believe in, to love, and to follow in the Prophet Jesus' teachings. Just as Christmas is a time for Christians to reflect on the legacy of the Prophet Jesus, Muslims too should take this as an opportunity to reflect on his guidance. My friends, there is nothing more beautiful than to wish your fellow Christian a merry Christmas and to share in their love for the Prophet Jesus. Be merry."[57]

---

[57] According to the late Sayyed Muhammad Hussein Fadlallah, who was one of the world's leading Islamic scholars: "Celebrating the birth of Christ should be in the same manner that the *Quran* celebrated his birth. The Glorious *Quran* did not detail the birth of any sacred person in the way it did when it talked about Christ, as one of God's greatest signs, especially in the *Surah* of *Mariam* (Mary) who is considered as one of the purified saints...Thus, dear loved ones, I want to say to all our brothers that it is not wrong to celebrate the birth of Christ. On the contrary, we encourage you to do so, for he is one of *Allah's* Messengers, but we have to observe our traditions in the process. Let us meet on Christmas or New Year's Eve and read the *Surah* of *Mariam*...We would like to emphasize, dear brothers and sisters, that *Allah* wants us to be joyful at the times of *Eids* (holidays), but it should be a spiritual and humanistic joy, full of love that we offer to our children and fellow human beings."[VI]

Is Listening to Songs and Music Permissible?

A man from the crowd yelled: "*Muntik*, what do you think of song and music?"

"Do not ask of him what we have already taught you! Musical instruments and singing are strictly forbidden," said *Sooilfahim*.

"*Sooilfahim*, it surprises me that you take such a firm stance on this issue. I am sure you are aware that many scholars do indeed permit singing and music."

"*Muntik*, I do not concern myself with the opinions of fools."

"Very well. *Sooilfahim* are there any *Quranic ayahs* that explicitly prohibit singing or music?"

"No *Muntik*, but there are certainly *ayahs* that imply that singing and music are forbidden:

> There are some human beings who purchase an enchanting diversion in order to lead people away from the way of Allah without having any knowledge, who hold the call to the Way of Allah to ridicule. A humiliating chastisement awaits them.[lxxxviii]

The words 'enchanting diversion' must be referring to singing."

"And on what basis do you think that this refers to singing?"

"*Muntik*, do you forget your history? Let me refresh your memory. This *ayah* is referring to the tactics that the *Quraysh* used to distract the Prophet *Muhammad's* early followers from his teachings."

"And what tactics did the *Quraysh* use as a distraction?"

"Is it not obvious? They would bring women to sing to the Prophet *Muhammad's* followers in hopes that it would draw their attention away from their newly found religious duties. Because of its potential to sway the pious from their religion, it has been prohibited."

"An interesting perspective. Let us evaluate this *ayah* together. At the very least, we can agree that this *ayah* refers to certain individuals who attempted to distract the Prophet *Muhammad's* followers from the way of God. Is this correct?"

"Yes *Muntik*."

"While you interpret enchanting diversion to refer to singing, I am sure there are other methods that could be used to distract others from their religious duties, would you not agree?"

"I suppose."

"How about statements of jest and spreading false rumors, could such tactics cause someone to go astray?"

"I suppose they could."

"What about enticing people to listen to long captivating tales of heroism and of ancient legends? Could this not distract someone long enough that they would miss their prayer?"

"Yes *Muntik*, this is possible."

"So we agree that there are other ways in which people may be lured away from their religious duties besides singing?"

"It seems that way."

"Now according to the *ayah*, what reason is their to punish these people that lure others using enchanting diversions?"

"Anyone who attempts to lead one of God's servants astray is worthy of condemnation."

"What if it was accomplished through the spreading of false rumors?"

"They too are worthy of condemnation."

"And of those who did it through telling long captivating tales of heroism and of ancient legends?"

"Them as well."

"It appears *Sooilfahim* that regardless how one leads God's servants astray, whether through singing, spreading rumors, or through telling tales, they are deemed unacceptable?"

"Of course!" yelled *Sooilfahim*.

"Then it appears that this *ayah* does not prohibit singing."

"And how do you figure that?"

"Is speaking in jest forbidden?"

"Certainly not *Muntik*."

"And what about telling tales, is this forbidden?"

"No."

"Of course not *Sooilfahim*. The *ayah* clearly implies that causing others to go astray from God's message is a punishable offense. It is not merely the device that was used to accomplish this distraction – otherwise, we would not have agreed that telling tales and that statements of jest, both of which we also agreed are capable of distracting someone from their religious duties, are not in themselves forbidden actions. Come now my friend, there are many other ways that one can be distracted from their religious duties. Plays, books, and poetry can all cause the mind to wonder for hours upon hours, as our imagination is lost within streams of imagery. Surely we do not take the position of forbidding plays, books, or poetry. *Sooilfahim*, let us waste no more time. What other proof do you have?"

"Very well. There is a *hadith* where the Prophet *Muhammad* said:

> From among my followers there will be some people who will consider illegal sexual intercourse, the wearing of silk (clothes), the drinking of alcoholic drinks and the use of musical instruments, as lawful.[lxxxix, 58]

Here the Prophet *Muhammad* is stating that from among his followers, some will go astray and practice that which is unlawful as lawful. Since musical instruments are mentioned in this *hadith*, it is clear that they are considered to be an unlawful Islamic practice."

"*Sooilfahim*, what about a tambourine, is that too forbidden?"

"Is it not a musical instrument? Of course it is forbidden."

"*Sooilfahim*, perhaps you are unaware but most scholars accept the permissibility of the tambourine[59] – an instrument well known to have been present during the time of the Prophet *Muhammad*. Its use is found in a number of *ahadith*:

> It was narrated from 'Aa'ishah that Abu Bakr (may Allaah be pleased with him) entered upon her and there were two girls with

---

[58] Though controversial, some scholars believe that only women are permitted to wear silk.

[59] While scholars are divided on the permissibility of musical instruments, it is largely accepted that the tambourine is exempt from this prohibition based on a number of *ahadith* depicting its common use at the time of the Prophet *Muhammad*.

her during the days of Mina beating the daff (tambourine), and the Prophet (peace and blessings of Allaah be upon him) was covering himself with his garment. Abu Bakr rebuked them, and the Prophet (peace and blessings of Allaah be upon him) uncovered his face and said, 'Leave them alone, O Abu Bakr, for these are the days of Eid.' That was during the days of Mina.[xc]

It was narrated that al-Rubayyi' bint Mu'awwidh ibn 'Afra' said: 'After the consummation of my marriage, the Prophet (peace and blessings of Allaah be upon him) came and sat on my bed as far from me as you are sitting now, and our little girls started beating the daff and reciting *ayah*s mourning my father, who had been killed in the battle of Badr. One of them said, 'Among us is a Prophet who knows what will happen tomorrow.' On that the Prophet said, 'Omit this (saying) and keep on saying the *ayah*s which you had been saying before.'"[xci]

It was narrated that Buraydah said: The Messenger of Allaah (peace and blessings of Allaah be upon him) went out on one of his military campaigns, and when he came back, a black slave woman came and said, 'O Messenger of Allaah, I vowed that if Allaah brought you back safe and sound, I would beat the daff before you and sing. The Messenger of Allaah (peace and blessings of Allaah be upon him) said, 'If you vowed that, then do it, otherwise do not do it.'' So she started to beat the daff, and Abu Bakr came in whilst she was doing so. Then 'Ali came in whilst she was beating the daff, then 'Uthmaan came in whilst she was beating the daff, then 'Umar came in and she threw the daff beneath her and sat on it. The Messenger of Allaah (peace and blessings of Allaah be upon him) said, 'The Shaytaan is afraid of you, O 'Umar. I was sitting and she was beating the daff, then Abu Bakr came in when she was beating the daff; then 'Ali came in when she was beating the daff; then 'Uthmaan came in when she was beating the daff, but when you came in, O 'Umar, she put the daff down.'[xcii]

At the very least, these three *ahadith* demonstrate that playing the tambourine is permissible during the *Eid*, a wedding, and when one returns after a prolonged absence. It appears the *ahadith* permitting the use of the tambourine are in clear contradiction to the *hadith* forbidding all musical instruments."

"No matter, there are certainly *ahadith* that speak of the evil of music:

> "The Prophet (pbuh) said, 'Verily Allah, Mighty and Exalted, sent me as a mercy to the worlds, and in order to eradicate string instruments, the flute and other pre-Islamic Pagan practices."[xciii]

Or does this *hadith* have some contradiction?"

"Let us figure it out together. Tell me *Sooilfahim*, do you think the *Quran* would be quite clear in outlining the purposes of the Prophet *Muhammad* or do you believe it would be ambiguous?"

"It must be clear as a cloudless night."

"I agree. I would find it very hard to imagine that God would not be transparent with His intentions in choosing the Prophet *Muhammad* to spread His message."

"I am glad we are finally finding some common ground *Muntik*!" exclaimed *Sooilfahim*.

"As am I! Now let us waste no more time. It appears that according to this *hadith*, the Prophet *Muhammad* was sent for three purposes. The first is as a mercy to mankind. What do you propose the Prophet *Muhammad* means by this?"

"Certainly it is by spreading the message of God that he is reminding those who have gone astray to return to His teachings," said *Sooilfahim*.

"Excellent! The *Quran* makes note of this mercy in *surah* 21, *ayah* 107:

> We have sent you forth as nothing but mercy to people of the whole world.[xciv]

And what of the second purpose? What Pagan practices did Islam eradicate?"

"Is this not also clear *Muntik*? Islam forbid the burial of unwanted female infants[60], gave women the right to their own dowry, forbid the worshipping of idols, and much more!"

---

[60] According to Islamic sources, pre-Islamic Arabia was corrupted with the practice of infanticide - particularly of females. Since females were seen as both a social and economic burden, they were regarded as more of a liability than of a male offspring. It is important to mention that while the practice of infanticide is found within the *Quran* and the *ahadith*, its prevalence remains a topic of debate among scholars. A fully developed and readily utilized written language did not exist at the time of pre-Islamic Arabia. Therefore, scholars have had to rely on Islamic sources

"I must say this all sounds to be correct. The *Quran* makes mention of everything you have just said. It condemns the killing of infants:

> When any of them is told about the birth of a female his face turns dark, and he is filled with suppressed anger, and he hides himself from people because of the bad news, thinking: should he keep the child despite disgrace, or should he bury it in dust? How evil is their estimate of Allah![xcv]
>
> And when the girl-child buried alive shall be asked: for what offence was she killed?[xcvi]

It grants women their own dowry:

> Give women their bridal-due in good cheer (considering it a duty); but if they willingly remit any part of it, consume it with good pleasure.[xcvii]"

And it forbids the worshipping of idols:

> None whom they had associated with Allah in His Divinity will intercede on their behalf; rather, they will disown those whom they had set up as Allah's associates in His Divinity.[xcviii]

Perhaps most importantly, the *Quran* says that all men and women are judged according to the law of God – their tribal status will not spare them from their wrongdoings:

> Then We revealed the Book to you (O Muhammad!) with Truth, confirming whatever of the Book was revealed before, and protecting and guarding over it. Judge, then, in the affairs of men in accordance with the Law that Allah has revealed, and do not follow their desires in disregard of the Truth which has come to you. For each of you We have appointed a Law and a way of life. And had Allah so willed, He would surely have made you one single community; instead, (He gave each of you a Law and a way of life) in order to test you by what He gave you. Vie, then, one with another in good works. Unto Allah is the return of all of you; and He will then make you understand the truth concerning the matters on which you disagreed.[xcix]

---

to gain information about the practice of infanticide during this time period.

It appears that the *Quran* is quite explicit with the purposes of the Prophet *Muhammad*."

"How could it not be *Muntik*?"

"And what of the third purpose? Where in the *Quran* does it say that the Prophet *Muhammad* was sent to eradicate musical instruments?"

"I do not recall of any *ayahs*."

"Very well. What about of the flute? Where in the *Quran* is the flute mentioned?"

"That too, I am unaware."

"Come now *Sooilfahim*, you cannot tell me that God would be so explicit with some of His purposes and not in others. Surely if this *hadith* is authentic as you claim it is, we should find some evidence to substantiate this claim of yours. How can something so important fail to be addressed in the *Quran*? I also find it most difficult to believe that spreading the message of God and abolishing practices of inequality and murder are somehow as worthy and important as eradicating musical instruments. There is nothing within the *Quran* or the *ahadith* that forbids singing or musical instruments. I tell you all to sing to your heart's content and let its sound sooth your soul."[61]

---

[61] Most Islamic scholars agree that the *Quran* does not prohibit musical instruments or singing. Scholars who are of the opinion that music is *haram* do not usually cite the *Quran* or the *ahadith;* this is simply because the *Quran* does not contain any *ayahs* prohibiting music or singing and because there is no unanimity regarding the authenticity of *ahadith* that do prohibit music and singing. Rather, these scholars support their claim on the basis of music's contents. In their view, music today is typically violent, sexually explicit, degrading towards women, and contains profound vulgarity. As these are all considered vices, one must stay away from them as they have the potential to lead one away from God. Unfortunately, such a view is both an overgeneralization and narrow-minded. To prohibit music on the grounds that some songs contain sexually explicit and vulgar language is no different than placing a prohibition on all novels because some may contain content that is considered unsuitable on religious grounds. It is obvious that Islamic scholars do not pass decrees banning all movies or books just because some contain content does not adhere to "Islamic guidelines." It is for this reason that some scholars, such as Dr. Shabir Ally and the late Sayyed Muhammad Hussein Fadlallah, are of the opinion that music, like any other pastime, is only to be avoided if its content draws one away from God or has a negative effect on the individual.

Are Tattoos Permissible?

A woman from the crowd yelled: "*Muntik*, what do you think of tattoos?"

"Do not ask of him what we have already taught you! Tattoos are *haram!*" said *Sakheef*.

"Correct me if I am wrong *Sakheef* but I do not recall anything in the *Quran* that prohibits tattoos."

"That is because their prohibition is found in a *hadith*," replied *Sakheef*.

"Then come and share with us this *hadith* so that we may evaluate it together."

"Very well:

> Allah has cursed those women who practise tattooing and those women who have themselves tattooed, and those women who get their hair removed from their eyebrows and faces (except the beard and the mustache), and those who make artificial spaces between their teeth for beauty.[c]

Are you satisfied?"

"Very much! Now as you know *Sakheef*, in Islam nothing is forbidden without reason. So tell us, why is tattooing *haram*?"

"Is it not obvious? The *hadith* clearly forbids it because it is considered an alteration of God's creation. Or do you think that altering God's creation to be a permissible act?"

"I am afraid I do not quite understand what you mean by altering God's creation. Do you mean this to be a physical change?"

"I do *Muntik*. The *Quran* clearly forbids altering God's creation:

> (O Prophet and his followers), turn your face singlemindedly to the true Faith and adhere to the true nature on which Allah has created human beings. The mould fashioned by Allah cannot be altered. That is the True, Straight Faith, although most people do not know.[ci]

Could it be any clearer?"

"*Sakheef*, this *ayah* is not referring to a physical creation but rather a spiritual one. Humans must recognize the nature of a single God as the Creator. If this *ayah* was referring to a physical attribute, it would have said the mould fashioned by Allah 'must not' be altered, but instead it says 'cannot. Now what other reasons do you have against tattoos?"

"The same *hadith* also mentions that because it is a form of beautification, it is prohibited."

"I presume this implies that any form of beautification, whether it be tattoos, or something else, is also forbidden on the grounds of them violating the code of modesty?"

"This is exactly what I mean, *Muntik*."

"And plucking of the eyebrows also falls under that which is considered beautification, is that correct?"

"Yes, the *hadith* I mentioned also includes plucking of the eyebrows."

"Tell me *Sakheef*, does Islam forbid one thing for one person but then allow it for another?"

"Of course not."

"Then I am afraid we have arrived at a problem *Sakheef*. Are tattoos a form of beautification?"

"Have we not already agreed that it was?"

"And what about plucking one's eyebrows?"

"Them as well."

"And what about clipping one's nails?"

"I suppose that too would fall under a form of beautification," muttered *Sakheef*.

"And what about cutting one's hair? Could that be considered a form of beautification?"

"Yes, it can."

"If all of these can be considered forms of beautification, why isn't clipping one's nails or cutting one's hair prohibited?"

"I do not know *Muntik*."

"Come now, there must be some other reasons."

"Tattoos are forbidden because they are a form of deception!" yelled *Sakheef*.

"I am afraid we are going in circles. By virtue of this argument, *Sakheef*, would you agree that anything that provides a form of deception would also be prohibited?"

"It would appear so," said *Sakheef*.

"What would cause more deception, a man with a tattoo on his arm or a woman wearing a cloak?"

"The latter."

"And is wearing a cloak forbidden, *Sakheef*?"

"It is not."

"How can this be? Not only is a cloak a form of deception, but it also causes more deception than a tattoo could ever hope to accomplish?"

"Tattoos invalidate one's *wudu*!"[62] yelled out *Sakheef*.

"Come now *Sakheef*, you must understand that as long as the water touches your skin, then you have completed your *wudu*. Besides, *wudu* is more than a physical cleanse – it is a discipline testing one's obedience to God and also symbolizes a spiritual cleanse before partaking in prayer. It is clear that the *Quran* places no prohibition on tattoos. Even the *hadith* outlining its prohibition appears to be deficient in reason."

---

[62] Before a Muslim performs prayer, they are required to perform *wudu* (ablution). This is a cleansing ritual where the mouth, nose, face and arms are washed. Some scholars hold the opinion that a tattoo prevents *wudu* from being properly performed since the tattoo acts as a barrier between the water and the skin. These same scholars apply the same logic for those who wear nail polish.

Is Growing a Beard Obligatory?

A man from the crowd yelled: "*Muntik*, what do you think of growing a beard?"

"Do not ask of him what we have already taught you! Males must grow beards. There is to be no further discussion!" cried out *Sooilfahim* in fury.

"Relax, *Sooilfahim*, so that we may both learn from each other. Do you believe that a beard is mandatory or that it is merely recommended?"

"It is a religious obligation!" yelled *Sooilfahim*.

"Then let us examine this at once! Does the *Quran* mandate males to grow a beard?"

"It does not," replied *Sooilfahim*.

"I did not think so. In fact there is only a single *ayah* in the *Quran* that mentions a beard and even then, it is only used to describe the Prophet Aaron:

> Aaron answered: 'Son of my mother! Do not seize me with my beard, nor by (the hair of) my head. I feared that on returning you might say: 'You sowed discord among the Children of Israel, and did not pay heed to my words.'[cii]

So tell us *Sooilfahim,* why do you believe that it is obligatory for Muslims to grow a beard?"

"This is what we have been taught in the *ahadith*."

"Please, share these *ahadith* so that we may all become more knowledgeable."

"Very well *Muntik*:

> Ibn Umar said, The Prophet said, 'Do the opposite of what the pagans do. Keep the beards and cut the moustaches short.'[ciii]

> Allah's Apostle said, "The Jews and the Christians do not dye (their grey hair), so you shall do the opposite of what they do (i.e. dye your grey hair and beards)."[civ]

His words are clear *Muntik*."

"It would appear so! Now tell us *Sooilfahim*, what do these two *ahadith* have in common?"

"Is it not obvious? The Prophet *Muhammad* is telling his followers to be unlike the Pagans, Christians, and Jews."

"And do you know why?"

"It is to help create an identity among the Muslims."

"This makes a great deal of sense. And would you agree that the Muslims at that time had succeeded in creating an identity for themselves?

"I would *Muntik*."

"Excellent. Now I assume that if the Muslims were told to grow their beards and keep their moustaches short, that the Pagans must have had short beards and long moustaches? Or perhaps they had neither beards nor moustaches?"

"It would appear so."

"If this is the case, is there any sense in continuing to apply this reasoning today?"

"What do you mean *Muntik*?"

"I think you will agree that today, Muslims are neighbored by all types of people. Some non-Muslims have beards and moustaches, while others do not. Would you agree?"

"I would."

"Then it appears that these reasons of establishing an identity and trying to be different than those around you no longer apply today.

"Perhaps *Muntik*, but there are many other reasons for growing one's beard."

"Then please, share with us that which you know."

"By shaving one's beard, you are essentially altering the creation of God, and this is *haram*. The *Quran* is quite clear on this matter:

> Truly it is only associating others with Allah in His divinity that Allah does not forgive, and forgives anything besides that to whomsoever He wills. Whoever associates others with Allah in His divinity has indeed strayed far away. Rather than call upon Him, they call upon goddesses, and call upon a rebellious Satan upon whom Allah has laid His curse. He said (to Allah): 'I will take to myself an appointed portion of Your servants and shall lead them astray, and shall engross them in vain desires, and I shall command them and they will cut off the ears of the cattle, and I shall command them and they will disfigure Allah's creation.' He who took Satan rather than Allah for his guardian has indeed suffered a manifest loss.[cv]

These *ayahs* clearly prohibit the disfiguring of God's creation."

"In order for us to make such conclusions, we must first understand these *ayahs*. This passage is reflecting on those who allow evil to guide their hearts instead of God. What is the main wrongdoing described in these *ayahs*?"

"As you have said, it is criticizing those who take the devil as their guide instead of God," said *Sooilfahim*.

"And what does the devil intend to do to those who take him as their guide?" asked *Muntik*.

"He will lead them astray."

"What else *Sooilfahim*?"

"He will lead them towards vain desires."

"Anything else?"

"He will cause them to cut off the ears of cattle."

"Correct *Sooilfahim*. When the *Quran* says: 'I shall command them and they will disfigure *Allah's* creation,' I do not believe it is referring to a physical disfigurement but rather a spiritual one. Even the mentioning of slitting the ears of cattle is at its core a spiritual deviation for we know that among the Arabian Pagans, there existed a superstition that by cutting the ears off of cattle they were honoring their deities. *Sooilfahim*, the *Quran* continuously emphasizes that we must not be led astray, that we must not let immoral desires take hold of us, and that we must never take idols or associate others with God for there is only One God. It is by deviating towards these vices that one disfigures God's creation."

"You have made your point *Muntik*, but as I have said before, there are many reasons for growing a beard and I have left the most important for last. Having a beard was simply the way of the Prophet *Muhammad*. We should follow his *sunnah*[63], or perhaps you have forgotten the Prophet *Muhammad's* words:

> Whoever revives my sunnah then he has loved me. And whoever loved me, he shall be with me in Paradise.[cvi]
>
> The Messenger of Allah (SAW) said: "Trim the mustache and leave the beard to grow."[cvii]

Surely you can understand this much."

"Of course, but you too must understand that the *sunnah* are not a religious obligation."

"Surely you are not saying we do away with the *sunnah*? yelled *Sooilfahim*.

"Far from it. I think it is a beautiful thing for someone to wish to emulate the Prophet *Muhammad*. But at what point does this emulation become excessive? It is believed that the Prophet *Muhammad* slept on his right side, ate with his right hand, and brushed his teeth with a *miswak*[64]. Are Muslims to follow these *sunnah* as well? There are over 100 *sunnah* pertaining to how the Prophet *Muhammad* drank, dressed, fasted, and even how he entered houses and mosques. Are all these to be emulated? Surely you can appreciate the beauty in human individuality and in one's own uniqueness. Acting in accordance with the *sunnah* is a marvelous gesture but you certainly cannot pass ill judgment on those who wish to have their own practices. So long as one is abundant in their own devotion to God, who are you to restrict their freedom?"

---

[63] In English, *sunnah* translates into habit, tradition, or practice. Within Islam, the term *sunnah* has been used to describe the life and the teachings of the Prophet *Muhammad*. (This is not to be confused with *ahadith,* which are the "sayings" of the Prophet *Muhammad*; *sunnah* refers to the "ways" of the Prophet *Muhammad*. It is by using the *ahadith* that one is able to derive the *sunnahs* of the Prophet *Muhammad*).

[64] A twig used to clean one's teeth.

Is the Hijab Obligatory?

A woman from the crowd yelled: "*Muntik*, what do you think of the *hijab*?"[65]

"Do not ask of him what we have already taught you! The *hijab* is an obligation decreed upon you by God Himself," cried out *Sakheef*.

"Please *Sakheef*, allow us to examine this together for this is a complicated matter," said *Muntik*.

"As you wish."

---

[65] The subject of head covering is among one of the most controversial and highly debated matters in Islam. No universal consensus exists among scholars in determining the religious decree surrounding the *hijab*. In the West, the *hijab* is often perceived as a sexist, oppressive, and archaic religious mandate. Such a view not only assumes that the *hijab* is an overwhelmingly imposed practice, but it also overlooks the historical, cultural, and personal context that accompanies an individual's decision to wear the *hijab*. According to Dr. Sahar Amer, author of *What is Veiling?* and a professor at the University of Sydney specializing in cross-cultural relations between Arab-Muslim societies and the West, "veiling is due to a variety of reasons, including social, political, cultural, and economic, as well as personal and spiritual ones. While some women indeed must wear the veil because it is imposed upon them by a society with a conservative reading of Islamic traditions, others wear it proudly out of deep piety and conviction that it is an Islamic prescription. Yet other women wear the veil as a political assertion of their national identity, or as an expression of their disappointment in the failure of Arab nationalism and of the postcolonial world, as a tool of resistance to Euro-American stereotypes and policies towards Muslims, or as a means of declaring their opposition to the commodification of women's bodies in Euro-American societies. Still others wear it for socio-economic reasons, either because it allows them to forego the expense of new clothes and a hairdresser, or because it gives them the confidence to go out in public, hold jobs, and become financially independent in a society only recently accustomed to having women mingle alongside men in public and work spaces. Perhaps the most important thing to understand about veiling is that there is not and has never been one singular reason for wearing hijab that one can consider valid for all peoples or all times or all societies. Variation is truly the norm."[VII]

"If we desire to understand the veil in Islam, I believe we must first understand a little of it's history. What can you tell us about this *Sakheef*?"

"My thought have escaped me *Muntik*."

"Then allow me to retrieve them. The veil is an ancient practice that has been used in different societies for different purposes. Some have used it to represent their martial status while others to show that they belong to a particular social class. Do you know what our Jewish brothers and sisters say about the veil?"

"I do not."

"Jewish law considers the veil a practice of modesty as a woman's hair is regarded as an immodesty. Now what about our Christian brothers and sisters?"

"That too I am unaware."

"The Bible states:

> Every man who prays or prophesies with his head covered dishonors his head. But every woman who prays or prophesies with her head uncovered dishonors her head—it is the same as having her head shaved. For if a woman does not cover her head, she might as well have her hair cut off; but if it is a disgrace for a woman to have her hair cut off or her head shaved, then she should cover her head. A man ought not to cover his head, since he is the image and glory of God; but woman is the glory of man. For man did not come from woman, but woman from man; neither was man created for woman, but woman for man. It is for this reason that a woman ought to have authority over her own head, because of the angels. Nevertheless, in the Lord woman is not independent of man, nor is man independent of woman. For as woman came from man, so also man is born of woman. But everything comes from God. Judge for yourselves: Is it proper for a woman to pray to God with her head uncovered? Does not the very nature of things teach you that if a man has long hair, it is a disgrace to him, but that if a woman has long hair, it is her glory? For long hair is given to her as a covering. If anyone wants to be contentious about this, we have no other practice—nor do the churches of God.[cviii]

Do you know *Sakheef* what Islam say about the veil?"

"This I do! *Surah* 24, *ayah* 31 states:

> And enjoin believing women to cast down their looks and guard their private parts and not reveal their adornment except that which is revealed of itself, and to draw their veils over their bosoms.[cix]

This *ayah* is proof that the *hijab* is mandatory!" exclaimed *Sakheef*.
"*Sakheef*, from what Arabic word is veil being translated from?"
"It is *hijab*."
"Not quite. The word being translated here is *khimar* – not *hijab*.[66] Do you know which *ayahs* contain the word *hijab*?"
"I do not *Muntik*."
"Then allow me to recite a part of their *ayahs*:

> And between the two there will be a barrier.[cx]

> And drew a curtain.[cxi]

> Ask from behind a curtain.[cxii]

> They say: "Our hearts are securely wrapped up against what you call us to, and in our ears is a heaviness, and between you and us there is a veil. And between you and us there is a veil.[cxiii]

> It is not given to any human being that Allah should speak to him except through revelation, or from behind a veil, or that a messenger (an angel) be sent to him who reveals to him by Allah's leave whatever He wishes.[cxiv]

In these *ayahs*, the word *hijab* is translated into barrier, curtain, and veil. In which of these *ayahs* is *hijab* referring to a piece of clothing that is worn to cover the head?"
"It appears none of them."
"And would you agree that in each of these *ayahs*, the word *hijab* is referring to some type of barrier that exists between two parties?"
'Yes *Muntik*, this appears to be the case."

---

[66] In vernacular Arabic, *hijab* is used to refer to the clothing that is used to cover a woman's hair and neck. In the *Quran*, the word *hijab* is not used to refer to this article of clothing but rather refers to a physical barrier. *Khimar*, which translates into "to cover," is however used to refer to an article of clothing traditionally worn that covers the head; in Arabic, *khimar* is also the word for alcohol as it covers one's judgment.

"But surely there exists *Quranic ayahs* on how men and women should dress[67], would you not agree?"

"Of course *Muntik*, such *ayahs* must exist."

"Then let us look at what the *Quran* tells us about how men and women should dress. By doing so, I believe we can come much closer to understanding Islam's position on the headscarf. Let us first turn our attention to *surah* 33, *ayah* 59:

> O Prophet, enjoin your wives and your daughters and the believing women, to draw a part of their outer coverings around them.[cxv, 68]

This *ayah* is referring to the *jilbab*, a long outer garment worn over a person's clothes. And what about the men you may ask? The *Quran* says:

> (O Prophet), enjoin believing men to cast down their looks and guard their private parts. That is purer for them. Surely Allah is well aware of all what they do.[cxvi]

Here the *Quran* instructs men to avoid looking at sights that may be inappropriate and also to guard that which is regarded as immodest.[69]

---

[67] One factor that complicates the understanding of dress codes in Islam is the existence of a number of words that each explains a different, though similar, type of clothing. For example, the *hijab* refers to a headscarf that covers the head and the neck. The *niqab* is clothing that covers the head, body, and face but spares the eyes. The *burqa* is similar to a *niqab* except that it has a screen that covers the eyes.

[68] The complete *ayah* reads: "O Prophet, enjoin your wives and your daughters and the believing women, to draw a part of their outer coverings around them. It is likelier that they will be recognised and not molested. Allah is Most Forgiving, Most Merciful." Whether held by Muslim scholars or critics of Islam, the view that this *ayah* commands Muslim women to cover themselves to avoid sexual assault from Muslim men is incorrect. According to one interpretation, slave women in that society were not covered with a veil. As slaves, they were often the targets of crude slurs and physical misconduct by the Pagans. In light of this situation, this *ayah* advised women to cover themselves with a *jilbab* so that they might be recognized as free women, thereby escaping the harassment that was often received by slaves. Should this be the proper interpretation and representation of the corresponding historical context, it becomes clear that the *jilbab's* purpose was limited to this particular situation and would not apply today.

[69] Many scholars believe that it is modest for males to cover themselves from their navel to their knees.

At this point, we have covered quite a bit of ground but I do not think we have come much closer to the main question at hand."

"No *Muntik*. It appears we have yet to reach the core of this issue."

"Then let us waste no more time. The heart of this issue comes from *surah* 24, *ayah* 31:

> And enjoin believing women to cast down their looks and guard their private parts and not reveal their adornment except that which is revealed of itself, and to draw their veils over their bosoms.[cxvii]

What is the Arabic word that veils is being translated from?"

"It is *hijab!*" exclaimed *Sakheef*.

"Not quite my friend. As we I have mentioned before, the *Quran* does not use the word *hijab* to refer to an article of clothing. The word translated here is *khimar*."

"Whether it is called *hijab*, *khimar*, or something else is of no matter. The message is the same."

"*Sakheef*, what does this *ayah* say regarding a woman's modesty. Does it not recommend the same rules as those asked of men?"

"It does *Muntik*."

"But it also asks women to cover their chest with their veils. Is this correct *Sakheef*?"

"It is."

"For us to truly understand this *ayah*, we must first understand what a *khimar* is. The *khimar* is an article of clothing that was worn by the women of Arabia, which covered the head and would extend down the back. Now it was part of the fashion that some women did not cover the upper parts of their chest. With this in mind, we can now understand the meaning of this *ayah*. The *ayah* is not commanding women to wear the *khimar* but rather is instructing them to take the part of the *khimar* that hangs behind them and to place it in front of them in order to cover the part of their chest that was often left bare."

"Even if this is the case *Muntik*, the *Quran* clearly mentions women wearing the *khimar*. Is this not proof enough that it is mandatory?"

"Not quite *Sakheef*. As you may know, the *khimar* is not an Islamic article of clothing. In fact, women long before the advent of Islam wore the *khimar*. Would you agree that at the very least, this *ayah* is stating that women use the *khimar* to cover their chest?"

"It would appear this way."

"And does this *ayah* directly mandate the wearing of the *khimar*, or is it, as we have discussed, saying to use the extension of the *khimar* to cover the front part of their bodies?"

"The latter *Muntik*."

"Are there any other *ayahs* in the *Quran* that you wish to bring forward on this matter *Sakheef*?"

"There are no other *ayahs*."

"My friends, what you should be sure of are the *Quran's* guidance on modesty that it enjoins on both men and women. Modesty is often viewed solely on how you dress, but let me remind you that your character better represents modesty than do the clothes on your back. Modesty is not just physical – it is spiritual. Be humble to your neighbors and leave your arrogance far away.

"There is no compulsion in religion. No one should force another into doing or wearing something that does not come from his or her own heart. The most beautiful Muslim is the man and woman who follow God's laws out of their trust in Him – not those who are forced to. You may profess your beliefs, but do not impose them for demanding practice without faith is a great injustice to God."[70]

---

[70] There is a wide spectrum of opinion on the issue of what is modest for a woman with respect to the veil. While some believe wearing the *hijab* is religiously obligatory, others believe women are under no such compulsion in following what is seen as remnants of a cultural tradition. Others maintain that a veil, though not required, is recommended. As one of the most contested issues in Islam, it is unlikely that scholars will reach a universal consensus on the subject of the veil. Despite Western belief, the majority of women who wear the *hijab* do so voluntarily for a number of reasons, including those that are spiritual, cultural, and even political. Perhaps best summarized by Armenian-American journalist Liana Aghajanian, "the headscarf has been banned, made mandatory, hailed as a symbol of religious virtue, accepted as a means of controlling female sexuality, and politicized by governments and colonizers across the world. Manipulated and misinterpreted, it is seen as both a sign of liberation and imprisonment, of progress and regression. It's a source of friction both outside and inside the communities that wear it."[VIII]

What are the Boundaries of Gender in Marriage?

A woman from the crowd yelled: "*Muntik*, what do you think of marriage?"

"Do not ask of him what we have already taught you! In Islam, a Muslim man may marry a Jewish, a Christian, or a Muslim woman but a Muslim woman may only marry a Muslim man. There are no exceptions," cried out *Sooilfahim*.

"Why is this, *Sooilfahim*?" asked *Muntik*.

"Surely *Muntik* you do not wish to challenge a tradition that is older than the both of us?"

"I do not wish to challenge, but only to understand. There are two *ayahs* in the *Quran* that I believe may help us to learn a little more about marriage in Islam. The first is *surah* 2, *ayah* 221:

> Marry not the women who associate others with Allah in His Divinity until they believe; for a believing slave-girl is better than a (free, respectable) woman who associates others with Allah in His Divinity, even though she might please you. Likewise, do not give your women in marriage to men who associate others with Allah in His Divinity until they believe; for a believing slave is better than a (free, respectable) man who associates others with Allah in His Divinity, even though he might please you.[cxviii, 71]

According to this, should a Muslim woman marry a believing man who is a slave or a *mushrik* man who is free?"

"This *ayah* clearly prefers one's faith over one's social class."

"And what about the Muslim man? Is he to marry a believing woman who is a slave or a *mushrik* woman who is free?"

---

[71] In Arabic, the word *mushrik* (plural, *mushrikeen*) is used to describe individuals who associate others with God's divinity. Specifically, it refers to idolatry or polytheism. In this *ayah*, *mushrikeen* is translated into "who associates others with Allah."

"The answer is the same as before. The believing woman who is a slave is more honorable."

"This appears to be the case *Sooilfahim*. Now there is another *ayah* that discusses the issue of marriage. Let us look at *surah* 5, *ayah* 5, which says:

> This day all good things have been made lawful to you. The food of the People of the Book is permitted to you, and your food is permitted to them. And permitted to you are chaste women, be they either from among the believers or from among those who have received the Book before you, provided you become their protectors in wedlock after paying them their bridal-due, rather than go around committing fornication and taking them as secret-companions. The work of he who refuses to follow the way of faith will go waste, and he will be among the utter losers in the Hereafter.[cxix]

It is believed that this *ayah* abrogated *surah* 2, *ayah* 221. Therefore we are left with the guidance of *surah* 5, *ayah* 5, which states that a Muslim man is permitted to marry a Christian or a Jewish woman."

"This is what I have been telling you *Muntik*! This *ayah* is only making an exception for men – not women. How can you believe that Muslim women are also permitted to marry Christian or Jewish men when the *ayah* clearly only gives this exception to men?"[72]

"But could we also not look at this in a different way *Sooilfahim*?"

"What do you mean *Muntik*?"

"Perhaps by permitting men the *Quran* is also indirectly permitting women."

"But *Muntik*, do you not think that if the *Quran* was also to extend this right to women that it would have mentioned it explicitly, thereby making it clear?"

---

[72] Essentially every major school of thought of Islam upholds the ruling that Muslim men may marry women belonging to the "people of the book." It is believed that if men had to be given special permission, by way of the *Quran,* to marry from the "people of the book" then women too would need to be granted this same permission. Because there is no *ayah* in the *Quran* that explicitly extends this right to women, scholars have held the belief that women may only marry men who are Muslim.

"Could I not say the same about its prohibition *Sooilfahim*? If God truly intended to prohibit women from marrying from the 'people of the book' would He not have made it clearer?"

"*Muntik*, do you wish to challenge tradition?"

"Far from it! I am merely trying to understand what has been practiced for so long. As we have discussed before, Islam does not send decree without reason. Why do you believe the *Quran* places this restriction on women and not men?"

"Isn't it obvious? The children must be raised Muslim and since mothers have more influence over their children than their fathers do, Muslim women must only marry Muslim men."

"If this is the case, shouldn't women be the ones to marry from the 'people of the book' and not men? If we accept your view that mothers will have more influence over their children than their fathers, wouldn't the children of a Muslim man married to a non-Muslim woman be more like the mother?"

"They would *Muntik*."

"It is clearly permissible for a Muslim man to marry a non-Muslim woman, yet it appears with your logic this would result in a child who is less Muslim than a union, that in your view is prohibited, between a Muslim woman and a non-Muslim man."

"You miss a very important point *Muntik*. You fail to recognize that children inherit the religion of their fathers – not their mothers."

"*Sooilfahim*, I am afraid this view is problematic. What does it matter if a child inherits his father's religion if there is still worry that his non-Muslim mother will have more influence over the children? Perhaps you remain unconvinced. Tell me, what makes a Muslim a Muslim?"

"What do you mean?"

"What separates a Muslim from a non-Muslim? Is it not the Islamic creed, which professes the belief in only One God and that the Prophet *Muhammad* is His messenger?"

"Yes *Muntik*, this is correct."

"And what about the Christian? What makes a Christian a Christian, is it not their acceptance of the Christian creed?"[73]

---

[73] Over the course of Christianity, different creeds have developed with the most popular and widely accepted being the *Nicene* Creed.

"Indeed."

"And what would you say of the Muslim who did not accept the Islamic creed, or of the Christian who did not accept the Christian creed? Could they be called Muslims or Christians if they do not uphold the most basic tenet of their faith, the core of their religion?"

"I do not see how they could."

"It appears that at the very least, religion requires a conscience affirmation. Would you agree with this?"

"It appears this way."

"*Sooilfahim*, with all that has been said how can you believe that religion is inherited when it is clear that theological doctrines require a personal integration within the human soul in order for them to be transformed into faith? A baby born of a Muslim man is as Christian as a baby born of a Christian man is Muslim.

"Tradition has told us that a Muslim man may marry a Jewish, a Christian, or a Muslim woman but the same right does not apply to a Muslim woman. My friends, God indeed wishes to preserve His guidance and blessings by asking you to marry and celebrate His teachings with your spouses and children. But let me ask you, how close to God is the couple who marry and inherit nothing more than their family name and some religious customs? Are their children better off than the household where only the mother is a Muslim but whose son and daughter embrace God and the Prophet *Muhammad* with all of their hearts?

"Marriage is more than just a means of spreading God's message - it is a relationship that sets the foundation for the institutionalization of a family. Interfaith homes may lead to marital instability, but what marriage isn't vulnerable to dispute? Let God, love, and respect guide your souls."

Were the Prophets Infallible?

A woman from the crowd yelled: "*Muntik*, what do you think of the prophets and sin?"

"Do not ask of him what we have already taught you! No one is without sin," said *Sooilfahim*.

"As believers in God and His loyal servants, your bodies are kept warm by recounting their miracles and the hardships they endured. The Prophet Job lost his health, family, and possessions while the Prophet Abraham was tossed into a fire for asserting that there was only one true God. These displays of ever-lasting faith and piety lead many of you to wonder if their character ever emulated anything other than complete righteousness. I should think it only natural that you ask yourselves if the prophets ever sinned."

"Of course the prophets have sinned, *Muntik*![74] There is ample evidence of this in the *Quran*," yelled out *Sooilfahim*.

"Then let us waste no more time. Should we find an *ayah* in the *Quran* that demonstrates that the prophets had sinned, I will have learned a great deal from you. But before we begin, I think it is important for us to define what we mean by sin. Surely we do not want to label a prophet's actions as sinful unless we understand the meaning of the word."

"This seems to be the way we should proceed."

"Excellent. Now would you agree that what is sinful is also immoral?"

---

[74] Islamic opinion on the infallibility of the prophets generally falls into one of three groups. The first is that the prophets were completely sinless, though opinion varies on whether the prophets were incapable of sinning as opposed to choosing not to sin. The second group believes that the prophets did not commit major sins (such as idolatry, polytheism, or murder) but were capable of committing minor sins; of note, many scholars believe that minor sins, such as jealousy, should be avoided but are not necessarily punishable. Lastly, a minority view believes that the prophets were capable of both major and minor sins.

"Certainly. A man who has committed a sin has indeed done something immoral."

"Would you also agree that a sinful action is one which requires intention?"

"I am not sure what you mean by this," replied *Sooilfahim*.

"Let us imagine you set out to buy bread. With the loaf in hand, you find yourself engaged in a long conversation with the baker. After some time, you break your engagement with the baker and make your way home, unaware that you have forgotten to pay for your bread. Do you consider yourself having stolen the bread?"

"Absolutely not! How could anyone dare call me a thief? I had every intention of paying for the bread."

"Precisely, *Sooilfahim*. It is for this reason that we define stealing as intentionally taking what is not yours without permission. However, as you mentioned, your intention was not to steal and should you have remembered that the loaf of bread was unpaid for, you would have gladly compensated the baker. Now let us instead assume that you remembered you had not paid for the bread yet proceeded to leave anyway. Is this sinful?"

"It is indeed sinful."

"This is what I meant to demonstrate with the word intention. It is a person's intention that allows us to recognize an action that is sinful from that which is sinless. Could we also extend this to morality? To intentionally sin is to act immorally?"

"This makes a great deal of sense *Muntik*."

"I believe it is now possible for us to properly examine what the *Quran* says about the prophets and to determine if they have committed acts of sin."

"Very well. We will start with the Prophet Adam. As you are well aware, *Muntik*, the Prophet Adam had committed a grave sin when he ate from the forbidden fruit. The *Quran* states:

> And We said: "O Adam, live in the Garden, you and your wife, and eat abundantly of whatever you wish but do not approach this tree or else you will be counted among the wrong-doers." But Satan caused both of them to deflect from obeying Our command by tempting them to the tree and brought them out of the state they were in, and We said: "Get down all of you; henceforth, each of you is an enemy of the other, and on earth you shall have your abode and your

> livelihood for an appointed time." Thereupon Adam learned from his Lord some words and repented and his Lord accepted his repentance for He is Much-Relenting, Most Compassionate.[cxx]

Is this not clear proof for you *Muntik*?"

"*Sooilfahim*, why do you believe that the Prophet Adam sinned?"

"Do you take me for a fool *Muntik*? I consider it a sin to disobey the command of God."

"I am afraid it is not that simple. Are you familiar with the concepts of *al-amr al-mawlawi* and *al-amr al-irshadi*?"

"I am not *Muntik*."

"You see, *al-amr al-mawlawi* refers to commands that are mandatory. Failure to act according to these orders is considered sinful and is therefore a punishable offense. On the other hand, *al-amr al-irshadi* refers to commands that are not obligatory but rather advisory in nature. One is free to neglect such advice, but doing so may very well result in unfortunate consequences. Tell me *Sooilfahim*, when it comes to murder, which type of command do you believe this falls under?"

"It must be *al-amr al-mawlawi*. Murder is a grave sin and is certainly a punishable offense."

"And what about stealing?"

"This too must be *al-amr al-mawlawi*. A thief is certainly worthy of God's wrath."

"What would you say about visiting the sick?"

"I must say, I cannot think of anything that requires us to tend to the sick," replied *Sooilfahim*.

"So this would not fall under *al-amr al-mawlawi*?"

"Not to my knowledge *Muntik*."

"But it was a *sunnah* of the Prophet *Muhammad*, was it not?"

"Indeed it was."

"Then would you advise your people to tend to the sick?"

"I certainly would."

"And if they did not, should they be fearful of any punishment?"

"None at all."

"So would you categorize a command asking to tend to the sick as *al-amr al-irshadi*?"

"Indeed *Muntik*."

"And what about the man who is sick and needs medicine but refuses to take them, should he be punished?"

"While God tells us that we should take care of ourselves and avoid harming the soul, I should find it difficult to judge this man's action as a sin."

"So he would be free from divine punishment?"

"Of course *Muntik*."

"Do you think this man may suffer from his decision?"

"Certainly. By choosing not to take his medicine, he is jeopardizing his health."

"What would you tell this man if he were right in front of you?"

"I would advise him to take his medicine and to watch his health."

"And if he does not comply with your wishes *Sooilfahim*?"

"Then he will be responsible for his own consequences."

"*Sooilfahim*, this is what is meant by *al-amr al-irshadi*. Such commands are advisory in nature and not obligatory. God advises His servants so that they may succeed and flourish. By following God's guidance, one will benefit greatly. While you are free to ignore God's advice, you will be responsible for the consequences. It is this principle that we must apply to the story of the Prophet Adam. God did not forbid the Prophet Adam from eating from the tree, but rather advised him not to. When he acted against God's guidance, the Prophet Adam committed *tarke awla*, that is, he abandoned that which was better."

"How can you say that *Muntik*, when God Himself tells the Prophet Adam that if he approaches the tree, he will be among the wrong-doers?"

"The Arabic word translated into wrong-doers is *al-zalimeen*, which in the context of this *ayah* may perhaps better be translated as 'those who commit injustice or harm upon themselves.' By eating from the tree, the Prophet Adam and Eve had indeed done themselves a great injustice as they were cast out of paradise and placed onto Earth."

"But *Muntik* do you forget that the Prophet Adam sought forgiveness from God? Surely one does not offer repentance unless he has sinned."

"*Sooilfahim*, let us imagine that you are the commander of an army. Because of your loyalty, the king has decided to bestow upon you a family heirloom, his most prized possession. How would you feel?"

"I would be honored."

"And suppose you became careless and lost the heirloom, how would you feel?"

"Quite awful *Muntik*."

"And if the king asked you how you were enjoying the heirloom, how might you reply?"

"I would offer my apologizes for losing his most prized possession."

"Even though he had given it to you?"

"I fail to see how this matters *Muntik*. Even though the heirloom became my possession, I had done him a greater disservice than I had done myself by failing to guard it."

"Do you think his disappointment would be greater with you considering you are one of his most loyal servants?"

"Of course. Is it not natural to expect more from those that you regard close to your heart?"

"I agree *Sooilfahim*, and this is precisely why the Prophet Adam repented and asked God for His forgiveness. Just as you felt guilty for losing your king's gift, the Prophet Adam too felt remorse for failing to guard God's most gracious gift – an abode in paradise. And just as your close loyalty to the king makes his disappointment in you greater, as too was God's dissatisfaction with the Prophet Adam for he was God's first human creation whose character was befitting to serve as the first prophet and messenger for mankind. The Prophet Adam asked for God's mercy not because he had sinned, but because a man of his high stature had failed to welcome God's advice and guard His gift of paradise."

"But *Muntik*, if Prophet Adam had not sinned, then why did God punish him by banishing him to Earth?"

"Remember what we have said *Sooilfahim*. The man who did not take his medicine will not be punished by God, but will surely suffer the consequences of his actions with worsening health. The same is true of the Prophet Adam. God did not punish the Prophet Adam by sending him to Earth, rather these are the consequences of his actions. Tell me, does God continue to punish the person whose repentance He accepts?"

"Of course not. Anyone who seeks forgiveness and gains God's acceptance will be showered with God's affection."

"This is precisely why we cannot view the Prophet Adam's placement on Earth as a punishment. The *Quran* tells us that God accepted his repentance, yet the Prophet Adam was not placed back in paradise."

"Very well *Muntik*, you have made your point. But I assure you the *Quran* has other examples that I am sure you will find harder to defend. Do you recall the story of the Prophet Moses when he murdered one of pharaoh's men? The *Quran* recounts this incident:

> "As for me, they hold the charge of a crime against me. I fear they will put me to death."[cxxi]

The Prophet Moses himself is admitting to his sin by calling his action a crime."

"*Sooilfahim*, allow me to recount the story for our friends. The incident is referring to an altercation between an Israelite and an Egyptian. The Israelite asked the Prophet Moses for help. When the Prophet Moses intervened, he struck the Egyptian with such a force that it killed him."

"Do not forget *Muntik* that the next day, the Prophet Moses fled to escape persecution from pharaoh for murder."

"*Sooilfahim*, many times we fear unjust retribution, though our hearts are free from sin. The Prophet Moses fled, not because he was guilty of any crime, but because he feared unjust retribution by the hands of the pharaoh. This is precisely why the Prophet Moses says 'they hold the charge of a crime against me.' Now, *Sooilfahim*, what did we decide about sin?"

"That to commit a sin is to commit an immoral act."

"And what does immorality require?"

"We agreed that it must be intentional."

"Precisely. And did the Prophet Moses intend on killing the man?"

"No *Muntik*, that was not his intention."

"If he did not intend to kill the man, how can we say that the Prophet Moses had sinned? Spiritually, the Prophet Moses was free from sin."

"And do you have similar words for the Prophet Noah, who after sinning asked God for forgiveness?"

"What sin do you charge the Prophet Noah with?"

"The one written in the *Quran*:

> And Noah called out to his Lord, saying: 'My Lord! My son is of my family. Surely Your promise is true, and You are the greatest of those who judge.' In response Noah was told: 'Most certainly he is not of your family; verily he is of unrighteous conduct. So do not ask of Me for that concerning which you have no knowledge. I admonish you never to act like the ignorant ones.' Noah said: 'My Lord! I take refuge with You that I should ask you for that concerning which I have no knowledge. And if You do not forgive me and do not show mercy to me, I shall be among the losers.'[cxxii]

Does God not admonish the Prophet Noah for his request to show mercy to his son despite not being a believer?"

"Just as the Prophet Noah asked God to forgive his son, a disbeliever, the Prophet Abraham did the same:

> After it has become clear that they are condemned to the Flaming Fire, it is not for the Prophet and those who believe to ask for the forgiveness of those who associate others with Allah in His Divinity even if they be near of kin. And Abraham's prayer for the forgiveness of this father was only because of a promise that he had made to him. Then, when it became clear to him that he was an enemy of Allah, he dissociated himself from him. Surely Abraham was most tender-hearted, God-fearing, forbearing.[cxxiii]

The Prophet Noah asks God to save his son from the great flood while the Prophet Abraham asks for forgiveness on behalf of his father. Despite their efforts, God reminds them that those for whom they seek refuge do not believe in Him and are therefore unworthy of His forgiveness and mercy. Surely you do not view a person's natural love for their kin as sinful."

"If it was not a sin, why did they ask for forgiveness?" cried out *Sooilfahim*.

"Did the Prophet Adam not ask for forgiveness even though he did not sin? You must realize that as prophets, they are held to the highest of standards. Because of their love and devotion to God, they seek forgiveness for even the slightness display of weakness in their character. This is not because they believed that they have sinned, but rather because God had bestowed upon them the greatest honor that a human can achieve. Prophethood. As prophets, they are role models for all of mankind and therefore must maintain the highest spiritual and intellectual consciousness. Do not forget that even Satan admitted he will have no power over God's most loyal servants:

> Satan said: "My Lord, then grant me respite till the Day that they are raised up." He said: "You are of those who have been granted respite till the Day whose Hour I know." (Iblis) said: "By Your glory, I shall mislead them all except those of Your servants, the chosen ones from amongst them."[cxxiv]

The prophets are a blessing to mankind. Strive to reach the moral integrity and spiritual perfection displayed by the prophets. Surely this is most pleasing to God."

Defeat

Left without anything to say, the *Motheyeen* were finally defeated. Their control over the people had been lost and their power diminished. The three-cloaked men had no choice but to leave the land. Their hand of influence had been severed and could never take hold of the people again. The *Motheyeen* disappeared into the crowd, never to be seen or heard from again.

Part Four – A New Embrace

Who (what) is Allah?

A woman from the crowd yelled: "*Muntik*, speak to us of *Allah*!"

"My friends, they ask you who *Allah* is and why you offer Him worship but refuse to praise God. I answer you, the difference between *Allah* and God is the same as that of *Shaitan* and Satan. Both are equal in meaning and differ only because of man's various tongues. *Shaitan* is as Christian as Satan is Islamic. *Allah*[75] and God are no different. Both refer to God, but do so through different dialects."

---

[75] In Arabic, the word *Allah* is derived from *Al* and *Ilah*, which means "The God." Just as Arabic-speaking Christians use the word *Allah* to refer to God, English-speaking Muslims use the word God.

What is a Muslim?

A woman from the crowd yelled: "*Muntik*, speak to us of Muslims!"

"My friends, your people are many and extend far beyond what the eyes can see. How can you ask me to speak on all Muslims? There are a great many Muslims in this world, each with their own culture, religiosity, and personal beliefs. To attempt to speak of or describe all Muslims presupposes that you are a single and homogenous group of people.

"At the very core, a Muslim is one who believes in the Islamic creed – 'there is no God but God and *Muhammad* is the Prophet of God.' Apart from this oath, there is nothing that so clearly links all Muslims as one.

"This practice of commenting on Muslims as if they were a single people must be stopped. Ask not 'do Muslims…' but instead 'does Islam believe or teach…' for this method seeks to understand what a single system teaches as opposed to erroneously fusing countless individuals under the same roof."[76]

---

[76] Over the past decade, there has continued a practice of speaking about Muslims as if they can be placed into a single category. Strictly speaking, there is nothing that all Muslims share in common besides the belief in the Islamic creed. However, even this basic requirement of affirming one's belief in God is not always universally present. According to a 2003 poll by Harris Interactive, while 79% of respondents who identified as Catholics stated they believed in God, 8% of Catholics stated they did not believe in God; this number was higher among the Jewish group, where as many as 19% stated they did not believe in God.[X] It is essential to recognize that a universal Muslim identity simply does not exist for the very simple reason that it cannot exist. One's identity is a culmination of their race, gender, ethnicity, nationality, sexuality, culture, and perhaps most importantly their experiences. It is therefore unreasonable to assume that Muslims somehow share in all, or even in enough, of these attributes to justify viewing Muslims under a single lens.

Islamic God vs Judeo-Christian God

A woman from the crowd yelled: "*Muntik*, speak to us of the God of the Abrahamic religions!"

"My friends, Muslims are the sisters of Jews and Christians, just as they are your brothers. Islam considers Jews and Christians to be 'people of the book' who received revelations from the same God.

"As Muslims, there is no dispute whether or not the three Abrahamic religions share the same God. He is the Father of Judaism, Christianity, and Islam. When a Jew, a Christian, or a Muslim speaks to God your prayers are delivered to the same One.

"Judaism, Christianity, and Islam are one in the same. Each takes a different path but arrives at the same truth. This single truth is God Himself – the One."

The Islamic View on Jesus

A woman from the crowd yelled: "*Muntik*, speak to us of the Prophet Jesus and Islam!"

"My friends, the Prophet Jesus is the son of Mary and is among the most pious of mankind:

> And when the angels said: 'O Mary! Allah gives you the glad tidings of a command from Him: his name shall be Messiah, Jesus, the son of Mary. He shall be highly honoured in this world and in the Next, and shall be one of those near stationed to Allah.'[cxxv]

"Like your Christian brothers and sisters, you believe in the virgin birth of the Prophet Jesus, for the *Quran* says that God had sent the Angel Gabriel to Mary:

> (O Muhammad), recite in the Book the account of Mary, when she withdrew from her people to a place towards the east; and drew a curtain, screening herself from people whereupon We sent to her Our spirit and he appeared to her as a well-shaped man. Mary exclaimed: "I surely take refuge from you with the Most Compassionate Lord, if you are at all God-fearing." He said: 'I am just a message-bearer of your Lord, I have come to grant you a most pure boy.' Mary said: 'How can a boy be born to me when no man has even touched me, nor have I ever been unchaste?' The angel said: 'Thus shall it be. Your Lord says: 'It is easy for Me; and We shall do so in order to make him a Sign for mankind and a mercy from Us. This has been decreed.''[cxxvi]

> And also recall the woman who guarded her chastity: We breathed into her of Our spirit, and made her and her son a Sign to the whole world.[cxxvii]

"Like your Christian brothers and sisters, you believe in the miracles performed by the Prophet Jesus:

> 'And he will be a Messenger to the Children of Israel.' (And when he came to them he said): 'I have come to you with a sign from your Lord. I will make for you from clay the likeness of a bird and then I will breathe into it and by the leave of Allah it will become a bird. I will also heal the blind and the leper, and by the leave of Allah bring the dead to life. I will also inform you of what things you eat and what you treasure up in your houses. Surely this is a sign for you if you are true believers.[cxxviii]

"Like your Christian brothers and sisters, you believe that the Prophet Jesus spread the same message of God:

> And We sent Jesus, the son of Mary, after those Prophets, confirming the truth of whatever there still remained of the Torah. And We gave him the Gospel, wherein is guidance and light, and which confirms the truth of whatever there still remained of the Torah, and a guidance and admonition for the God-fearing.[cxxix]

> In their wake, We sent a succession of Our Messengers, and raised Jesus, son of Mary, after all of them, and bestowed upon him the Evangel, and We set tenderness and mercy in the hearts of those that followed him.[cxxx]

"Like your Christian brothers and sisters, you believe that the Prophet Jesus ascended to heaven and will one day return as the Messiah:

> (And it was part of His scheme) when Allah said: 'O Jesus! I will recall you and raise you up to Me and will purify you (of the company) of those who disbelieve, and will set your followers above the unbelievers till the Day of Resurrection. Then to Me you shall return, and I will judge between you regarding what you differed.[cxxxi]

"Just as there are similarities, you too will find differences. Unlike your brothers and sisters, you reject the notion of the holy trinity and do not attribute any divinity to him:

> People of the Book! Do not exceed the limits in your religion, and attribute to Allah nothing except the truth. The Messiah, Jesus, son of Mary, was only a Messenger of Allah, and His command that He conveyed unto Mary, and a spirit from Him (which led to Mary's conception). So believe in Allah and in His Messengers, and do not

> say: (Allah is a) trinity. Give up this assertion; it would be better for you. Allah is indeed just one God. Far be it from His glory that He should have a son. To Him belongs all that is in the heavens and in the earth. Allah is sufficient for a guardian.[cxxxii]
>
> And imagine when thereafter Allah will say: 'Jesus, son of Mary, did you say to people: "Take me and my mother for gods beside Allah?" and he will answer: "Glory to You! It was not for me to say what I had no right to. Had I said so, You would surely have known it. You know all what is within my mind whereas I do not know what is within Yours. You, indeed You, know fully all that is beyond the reach of human perception.[cxxxiii]

"Unlike your Christian brothers and sisters, you teach that the Prophet Jesus was only a prophet of God:

> The Messiah, son of Mary, was no more than a Messenger before whom many Messengers have passed away; and his mother adhered wholly to truthfulness, and they both ate food (as other mortals do). See how We make Our signs clear to them; and see where they are turning away![cxxxiv]
>
> "Verily I am Allah's servant. He has granted me the Book and has made me a Prophet and has blessed me wherever I might be and has enjoined upon me Prayer and Zakat (purifying alms) as long as I live."[cxxxv]

"Unlike your Christian brothers and sisters, you teach that the Prophet Jesus was not crucified:

> Then they schemed (against the Messiah), and Allah countered their schemes by schemes of His own. Allah is the best of schemers.[cxxxvi]
>
> And their saying: 'We slew the Messiah, Jesus, son of Mary', the Messenger of Allah – whereas in fact they had neither slain him nor crucified him but the matter was made dubious to them - and those who differed about it too were in a state of doubt! They have no definite knowledge of it, but merely follow conjecture; and they surely slew him not, but Allah raised him to Himself. Allah is All-Mighty, All-Wise.[cxxxvii]

"I ask you not to let these differences divide you! You are all brothers and sisters, torn away from your mother at birth and have come to see the world through different truths. Focus on what you share in common so that you may eat, drink, and live peacefully among one another."

The Islamic View on the Original Sin

A man from the crowd yelled: "*Muntik*, speak to us of the original sin!"

"My friends, the Bible teaches the Fall of Man. In Christian doctrines, it is considered a sin that the Prophet Adam ate from the forbidden fruit. He disobeyed God's order and fell victim to temptation. As a result, it is believed that all of mankind is born with sinful natures because of the sin of the Prophet Adam. It was only through the sacrifice of the Prophet Jesus that humanity's sins could be forgiven.

"In Islam, there is no concept of the original sin. The *Quran* teaches that the Prophet Adam asked God for His forgiveness, and that God accepted his repentance:

> Thereupon Adam learned from his Lord some words and repented and his Lord accepted his repentance for He is Much-Relenting, Most Compassionate.[cxxxviii]

"The *Quran* teaches that every individual is punished for their own sins and rewarded for their own good deeds:

> Everyone will bear the consequence of what he does, and no one shall bear the burden of another. Thereafter, your return will be to your Lord, whereupon He will let you know what you disagreed about.[cxxxix]

"The *Quran* teaches that it is the piety and love in your hearts that reaches God, not the blood of a sacrifice:

> Neither their flesh reaches Allah nor their blood; it is your piety that reaches Him.[cxl]

"The *Quran* teaches that even those who have committed grave sins need only open their hearts to God to receive His mercy:

> Tell them, (O Prophet): "My servants who have committed excesses against themselves, do not despair of Allah's Mercy. Surely Allah forgives all sins. He is Most Forgiving, Most Merciful.[cxli]

"Sin is unlike the color of your eyes or the shape of your face. It cannot be inherited and passed down from one generation to the next. Your sins are your own, just as are your good deeds. For the man who wronged his soul, it is only his piety that can pave the way towards redemption. As for the woman who opened her heart to the poor, it is her soul that God will shower with love and affection."

The Crescent Moon

A man from the crowd yelled: "*Muntik*, speak to us of the symbol of Islam!"

"My friends, each of the Abrahamic religions has a sign that has become associated with their faith. Your Jewish brothers have the Star of David while your Christian sisters have the Cross. In Islam, the Crescent Moon and the Star have been identified with the Islamic faith.[77]

"Despite the association between the crescent moon and Islam, let me affirm that Islam does not recognize this as the emblem for all Muslims. The moon and the stars are not to be worshipped and are not prescribed symbols from God. There are even those among you who have distanced yourself from these symbols fearing that it is reminiscent of the past.[78] So long as you do not worship that which is not to be worshipped, fear not unjust retribution."

---

[77] The history of the crescent moon and the star's introduction into Islam remains a matter of debate. While these symbols predate Islam by well over 1000 years, it is unknown when they first came into use. Historically, the crescent moon and star have been found on coins, tombstones, and flags. Some historians argue that Sultan Mustafa III of the Ottoman Empire first adopted the crescent moon in the 18th century. Others propose an earlier appearance, tracing its introduction back to the 15th century, when Sultan Mehmed II of the Ottoman Empire conquered the city of Constantinople. Whether the crescent moon was intended to only represent the Ottoman dynasty also remains a mater of debate.

[78] Since the practice of pre-Islamic Arabia concentrated on pagans and the worship of symbols and statues, some argue that symbols, such as the crescent moon and star, should not be attributed or integrated into the Islamic faith.

What is Ramadan?

A man from the crowd yelled: "*Muntik*, speak to us of the importance of *Ramadan*!"

"My friends, *Ramadan* is the ninth month of the lunar calendar and it begins with the sighting of the full moon. It is during this month that the Prophet *Muhammad* first received God's revelations.

"The *Quran* says:

> Believers! Fasting is enjoined upon you, as it was enjoined upon those before you, that you become God-fearing.[cxlii]

During the month of *Ramadan*, you are to abstain from the most basic human desires from sunrise to sunset. Though you may crave food, water, and intimacy you are to abstain from these desires until the sun descends below the horizon.

"This is a time where you must focus on your own spiritual development. You are to resist unlawful temptations, avoid disputes or conflicts, and practice forgiveness and compassion. Surely *Ramadan* is a discipline for your souls.

"You ask what is the importance of *Ramadan*, I tell you this holy month is a time to develop self-discipline and to cultivate your faith and spirituality in God. During your fast, you will endure some of the hardships shared by those who are unable to afford bread and water. Let this experience humble you.

"But what of those of you who are unable to fast? Recall, God does not wish to place unnecessary burdens upon His servants:

> Fasting is for a fixed number of days, and if one of you be sick, or if one of you be on a journey, you will fast the same number of other days later on. For those who are capable of fasting (but still do not fast) there is redemption: feeding a needy man for each day missed. Whoever voluntarily does more good than is required, will find it better for him; and that you should fast is better for you, if you only know.[cxliii]

"I tell you this month is a glamorous opportunity to strengthen your soul, releasing it from the clutches of your body's desires. Let moderation and discipline be the masters of your mind. *Ramadan* is a month of spiritual healing, so go and allow it to rejuvenate your faith in God."

The Sacredness of Churches

A child from the crowd yelled: "*Muntik*, speak to us of churches!"

"My friends, you all share the same God just as all life shares the same one Earth. Each man and woman have their own temple where they gather to worship and praise God; your Jewish brothers have the synagogue, your Christian sisters have the church, and Muslims have the mosque. Each of these places of worship serves as a House of God.

"There are those among you who believe that it is forbidden for a Muslim to enter a church.[79] You say this is because a church is not a House of God, while others say it is because a church contains statues.[80] Let me remind you that a church, like a synagogue, is as much a House of God as a mosque. The prayers of the 'people of the book' reach the same God as yours.

"When you offer praise to your Lord, is it not your prayer that reaches Him? Then why do you worry yourself with where you are standing if it is only your words that are most important to God? I

---

[79] With respect to Islamic jurisprudence, there are different Islamic schools of thought. Within Sunnism, the four main schools are the *Hanafi*, *Shafi'i*, *Maliki*, and *Hanbali*. Generally speaking, the *Hanafis* believe it is not permissible for a Muslim to enter a church. The *Shafi'is* take a slightly less restrictive approach and assert that it is only impermissible to enter churches that contain images. The *Hanbalis* maintain that while Muslims are permitted to enter churches, it is better if it is avoided.[XI]

[80] In an effort to dissuade early converts from reverting back to the practice of idol worshipping, the Prophet *Muhammad* forbade statues. Today, many scholars strictly adhere to this practice and believe that statues are prohibited. As a result, some Islamic schools of thoughts assert that Muslims are prohibited from entering any building that contains a statue (though exceptions do exist to this rule). Other scholars take a less restrictive approach and believe that so long as one does not worship a statue, then there is no prohibition in entering a building with a statue or even owning one.

tell you there is nothing more beautiful than to see men and women of different faiths worshipping under the same roof."

The Fate of non-Muslims

A woman from the crowd yelled: "*Muntik*, speak to us of the fate of non-Muslims!"

"My friends, I have heard many tales of the fate of non-Muslims in Islam. You say that non-Muslims are condemned to hell and have no place in heaven. You say that Muslims are guaranteed heaven and have no fear of hell. I ask these storytellers to tell us where they have gained this Godly knowledge.

"As God's servants, you have been made to understand the difference between that which is just and that which is unjust, and therefore are free to judge what is right and what is wrong. But what knowledge has God given you that you are worthy of judging salvation?

> Say: "O Allah, the Originator of the heavens and the earth, the Knower of the unseen and the seen, You it is Who will judge among Your servants concerning what they differed.[cxliv]

> (Know well, none has an exclusive claim to the Truth). [cxlv]

The *Quran* only describes those who deserve His grace and who deserve His wrath. That who pleases His grace is deserving of Reward and that who angers His grace is deserving of Punishment. The path towards salvation is described in the *Quran*:

> For all those who believe in Allah and in the Last Day and do good deeds – be they either believers, Jews, Sabaeans or Christians – neither fear shall fall upon them, nor shall they have any reason to grieve. [cxlvi, 81]

---

[81] Very little is actually known about the Sabaeans. Some believe that the Sabaeans lived in the south of the Arabian Peninsula while others place them in Iraq. In respect to their religion, difference in opinions also exists. It remains unclear whether they were closely related to the Jewish or Christian faith.

"And what of those who have never heard God's message, do you condemn them to a lifetime of misery? Are the teachings of God only for those who hear or read His message? Surely the other names of God include the All-Loving, the All-Merciful, and the All-Kind. His words and compassion are a blessing to all of mankind:

> He who follows the Right Way shall do so to his own advantage; and he who strays shall incur his own loss. No one shall bear another's burden. And never do We punish any people until We send a Messenger (to make the Truth distinct from falsehood).[cxlvii]

All men and women are to be judged on the same principles of justice and morals. Or do you think the good deeds of those unlike you will be wasted? Is God not the Lord of all mankind?

"There are those among you who believe that paradise is only reserved for the Muslim man and the Muslim woman. As proof, you offer the *Quran* as your witness:

> And whoever seeks a way other than this way a submission (Islam), will find that it will not be accepted from him and in the Life to come he will be among the losers.[cxlviii]

I say in return, do not misunderstand God's holy book. The way of Islam is the way of submission. The way of submission is the one who commits, submits, and whose actions reflect the truth.

"What do you say about the non-Muslim whose life was wholly dedicated to the justice and protection of men, women, children, and animals? Do you condemn him to hell because he did not submit to the laws of Islam? I tell you that Islam is not a religion of laws but a religion of love, compassion, and righteousness. I ask you, did the Prophet *Muhammad* preach laws or did he preach about equality, justice, and morality?[82] Why did *Bilal* and the Pagans of Arabia

---

[82] When asked what it means to be a Muslim, the knee-jerk response of many Muslims is often to explain the belief in the five pillars of Islam – namely faith, prayer, fasting, charity, and pilgrimage. While the five pillars of Islam is undeniably a core component of Islam, limiting the explanation of Islam to these practices fails to properly describe the religion. Islam is more than just a religion of laws. In fact, the requirements of Muslims to fast, give to charity, and perform the holy pilgrimage were not made obligatory until the *hijrah* in 622 CE, twelve years after

convert to Islam, was it because the Prophet *Muhammad* enjoined them to pray and to fast? No, it was the Prophet *Muhammad's* message of equality and teachings of justice that compelled those who listened to embrace Islam.

"Surely the non-Muslim who dedicates his life to serving, helping, and protecting others has submitted to Islam. Or do you think the Muslim whose only concerns are his own pleasures has done more for humanity?

"My friends, why did God create you? The *Quran* answers:

> I created the jinn and humans for nothing else but that they may serve Me.[cxlix]

And what purpose is there in serving God and in reciting prayer? The *Quran* answers:

> O mankind, serve your Lord Who has created you as well as those before you; do so that you are saved.[cl]

> (O Prophet), recite the Book that has been revealed to you and establish Prayer. Surely Prayer forbids indecency and evil. And Allah's remembrance is of even greater merit. Allah knows all that you do.[cli]

By invoking the name of God, you guard yourself against that which is harmful to you.

"I tell you that the purpose of religion is to be righteous. Do not believe that the righteous unbeliever who refrains from aggression is less worthy than the unrighteous believer who engages in aggression. What can be more pleasing to God than to watch His servant acting righteously?

"Do not claim to know who will enjoy the blessings of paradise or the torments of hell. This knowledge lies with God and God alone."

---

the Prophet *Muhammad's* first revelation; even prayer was not mandated until ten years after the Prophet *Muhammad* began preaching the message of Islam. This begs the question, if the Prophet *Muhammad* did not preach these basic laws at the inception of Islam, what was he preaching for the first ten years? Social reform.

The Religions of the Prophets

A woman from the crowd yelled: "*Muntik*, speak to us of the prophets and their religion!"

"My friends, they say that all prophets before the Prophet *Muhammad* were Muslim and followed Islam. I tell you these words are true, for the *Quran* teaches you:

> Abraham was neither a Jew nor a Christian; he was a Muslim, wholly devoted to God. And he certainly was not amongst those who associate others with Allah in His divinity.[clii]
>
> Moses said: 'My people! If you believe in Allah and are truly Muslims then place your reliance on Him alone.'[cliii]
>
> He has prescribed for you the religion which He enjoined upon Noah and which We revealed to you (O *Muhammad*), and which We enjoined upon Abraham and Moses and Jesus, commanding: 'Establish this religion and do not split up regarding it.' What you are calling to is very hard upon those who associate others with Allah in His Divinity. Allah chooses for Himself whomsoever He pleases and guides to Himself whoever penitently turns to Him.[cliv]

"Islam means submission, obedience, and peace.[83] Any person who submits to God is following Islam, just as any person who submits to God is a Muslim. Did the Prophet Abraham and Moses not submit themselves to God? Then how can you deny that they are among the most righteous of Muslims?

"If to be a Muslim means to submit to the Will and Laws of God, then is it not clear that all of God's servants are Muslim? Every Prophet of God belonged to the same brotherhood, serving the same purpose, and delivering the same message."[84]

---

[83] The word Islam comes from the word *aslam* and the root word *salema*, which means submission.

[84] It is important to recognize that the *Quranic* definition of a Muslim is different

than its vernacular use. The *Quranic* definition of a Muslim is simply one who submits. In Islam, prophets, from the Prophet Adam to the Prophet *Muhammad*, fit this *Quranic* description of a Muslim since they all submitted to God.

Becoming the Perfect Muslim

A child yelled out from the crowd, "*Muntik*, speak to us of becoming the perfect Muslim!"

"My friends, if you wish to become the perfect Muslim then you must strive in your religious duties. The perfect Muslim is the one who has faith in God. The perfect Muslim is the one who performs the five daily prayers. The perfect Muslim is the one who endures the hardships of the one-month fast. The perfect Muslim is the one who gives alms to those in need. The perfect Muslim is the one who embarks on the holy pilgrimage in the land of *Mecca*.

"If you wish to become the perfect Muslim, you must not only strive in your religious duties, but you must also strive in your humanitarian duties. The perfect Muslim is the one who feeds the poor. The perfect Muslim is the one who helps the weak. The perfect Muslim is the one who guides the naïve. The perfect Muslim is the one who clothes the naked. The perfect Muslim is the one who shelters the homeless. The perfect Muslim is the one who tends to the sick. And above all, the perfect Muslim is the one who cares for his parents – never underestimate the blessings of your mother.

"If you wish to become the perfect Muslim, you must not only strive in your humanitarian duties, but you must also strive in your personal duties. God does not like to see His servants suffer or to endure unnecessary hardships. Your life belongs to you and your Lord, so dedicate your time to Him but leave a portion to yourself and your own pursuits of happiness. Do not forbid yourself that which your soul desires. While you may be borrowing the Earth from your children, you also inherited it from your parents and therefore are entitled to a life of happiness and joy.

The Prophet *Muhammad* once said:

> 'No man is a true believer unless he desires for his brother that which he desires for himself.'

"The perfect Muslim is more than the father who dedicates his life to his religious duties or the mother who dedicates her life to her humanitarian duties. The perfect Muslim is also the one who strives in pursuing his own happiness."

Sunnis and Shias

A woman from the crowd yelled: "*Muntik*, speak to us of the *Sunnis* and the *Shias*!"

"My friends, the *Sunnis* and *Shias*[85] are two brothers that were raised in the same house, taught by the same master, and pursued the same destination but through different paths.

"Recall that what you call *Sunnis* and *Shias* today is only a result of political disagreement of over 1000 years ago. When the Prophet *Muhammad* passed, a new *caliph*[86] was set to emerge that would assume leadership over the *ummah*. Who was to become the next leader? It is with great sadness that this uncertainty escalated into a societal dilemma that soon divided the Muslim community forever.

"Those who believed that *Abu Bakr* rightfully assumed his role as the first *caliph* became known as *Sunnis*. And those who believed that *Imam Ali* should have been appointed as the first *caliph* became known as *Shias*. It is this difference of opinion between your ancestors that has despairingly split the Islamic community.

"Over time, this political difference paved the way towards greater segregation between the two groups, and ultimately the differences between *Sunni* and *Shia* Muslims outgrew this political issue of assigned leadership and eventually boiled over into religious differences.

---

[85] *Sunnis* make up over 85% of the world Muslim population, and make up the majority in many Muslim countries, such as Turkey, Saudi Arabia, Egypt, and Jordan. *Shia* Muslims are scarcer and are predominately found in Iran and Iraq and are also part of large minority groups in regions such as Yemen, Lebanon, and Bahrain.

[86] A *caliph* is the term given to the figurehead or leader of the Muslim community. This individual would be in charge of both the political and religious direction of the Islamic community.

"There are those among you who wish to further divide your *ummah*. I ask you, do you so quickly forget God's words? The *Quran* says:

> This community of yours is one community, and I am your Lord; so hold Me alone in fear. But people later cut up their religion into bits, each group rejoicing in what they have.[clv]

There is no glory or reward in dividing the religion of God. Or do you truly forget that the two of you share the same God?

"Both *Sunnis* and *Shias* believe that there is only God and that the Prophet *Muhammad* was the last Prophet and Messenger of God.

"Both *Sunnis* and *Shias* pray to their Lord five times a day, prostrating themselves before Him. Some Muslims pray with their arms by their sides while others prostate with their foreheads pressed against a *turbah*. [87] Do you take these differences to be worthy of is animosity between *Sunnis* and *Shias*? Surely it is the piety in your own hearts that concerns God.

"Both *Sunnis* and *Shias* fast from sunrise to sunset during the holy month of *Ramadan*. Some Muslims break their fast a few minutes after the other.[88] Do you consider the Muslim who breaks

---

[87] Two differences between *Sunnis* and *Shias* in prayer are the position of the arms and the use of the *turbah* (a clay rock). *Sunnis* fold their arms in front of their bodies while *Shias* place their arms along their sides. S*hias* also tend to prostrate with their foreheads pressed against a *turbah*. (It is interesting to note that some Muslims criticize *Shias* for the use of the *turbah*, claiming that it is both innovation and reminiscent of idol worshipping. Despite these claims, the use of the *turbah* is merely to reproduce the conditions in which the Prophet *Muhammad* prayed; the Prophet *Muhammad* would prostate with his forehead pressed against the earth, and therefore the *turbah*, which is made from clay, symbolizes that prostration). Considering both *Sunnis* and *Shias* follow different schools of Islamic law, it is not surprising that each has developed and follows different traditions. In fact, *Maliki*, one of the four main *Sunnis* schools of Islamic law, do not pray with their arms folded in front of their bodies.

[88] *Surah* 2, *ayah* 187 of the *Quran* describes when Muslims may break their fast. There is a difference of opinion among scholars as to the exact time described in the *Quran*. *Sunnis* believe that one must break their fast at sunset while *Shias* interpret *ayah* 187 as instructing Muslims to break their fast a few minutes after sunset, when the sky has become completely dark.

his fast earlier unworthy of God's praise? Surely it is the spiritual journey that pleases Him.

"Both *Sunnis* and *Shias* give *zakat*.

"Both *Sunnis* and *Shias* perform the *hajj*.

"I ask what differences can exist among you that overpowers these similarities?[89] Do not forget what God revealed to the Prophet *Muhammad* when he witnessed His servants fighting among each other:

> Hold fast together to the cable of Allah and be not divided. Remember the blessing that Allah bestowed upon you: you were once enemies then He brought your hearts together, so that through His blessing you became brothers. You stood on the brink of a pit of fire and He delivered you from it. Thus Allah makes His signs clear to you that you may be guided to the right way.[clvi]

If God commanded two peoples who were once enemies to stop fighting, what do you think He would say to those who were once brothers and sisters?

"You can choose to emphasize your differences but this will only lead to more division, or you can choose to emphasize your similarities which will undoubtedly lead to unity. I do not ask that you forget your histories or forgo the laws and practices that you have developed. This is your identity and nothing is more beautiful than the pride you display for your heritage. Go and discuss your differences with an open mind and an open heart. Speak with each other how you would like to be spoken to and do not be arrogant in your speech. Respect the differences of your brothers or sisters, or is it only suitable to tolerate the differences of your friend and of the stranger?

"The time for reconciliation is now. Love and embrace one another like a mother when she finds her lost child."

---

[89] There are many other differences that exist between *Sunnis* and *Shias*. However, there is also a great deal of misinformation and slander. For example, *Shias* are often charged with believing that the *Quran* has been altered, that the twelve *imams* are venerated as saints, and that *Imam Ali* is viewed as a prophet. Despite such accusations, none of these claims are mainstream within *Shia* ideology.

Part Five – Farewell

Muntik's Departure

The man from my father's stories, the wanderer from the desert, defeated the *Motheyeen* and restored our people to their rightful ways. The three-cloaked men were never seen nor heard from again, existing only in the distant memories of those affected by their tyranny. The *Motheyeen* inscribed promises of protection in their book of lies, but it was *Muntik* who revealed it was written in invisible ink. We were caged birds, lingering for a freedom that only *Muntik* could deliver. Ours souls were finally reunited with the land where we were born and bred, whose grass and dirt is well known to our hands and feet.

We asked *Muntik* to stay and become our leader, but he refused believing that he had still much to learn. But before leaving, *Muntik* left us with these final words of wisdom:

"You have quenched the thirst of this lonesome traveler
with talk of justice and virtue.
Allow me to share some final words of wisdom,
but do not let these words be short-lived like the passing of a cloud
during a storm.
Let my words dwell deep within your hearts and in that of your
children,
for I will read to you from the book of life.
These truths have been revealed since the beginning of time
and will remain until the end of eternity.

Your lips have been moistened from the cup of truth
and your minds liberated from the clutches of falsehood.
Sink back not into darkness
for you have journeyed into the light.
The wickedness of yesterday has been vanquished
and the reign of virtue has been restored.

The mind is man's greatest asset
bestowed by God as a glorious gift.
Do not abandon nor neglect it
for the soul requires it for guidance.
Each man is owner to his own mind so do not cast it aside
and blindly allow that of another to persuade you.
Discover where hypocrisy lays
and challenge its authority.
Find the door of deception
and let your mind unlock it.
Above all, think for yourselves
and let no man think for you.

Reason is the highest truth
and is among the greatest of virtues.
It alone will lead you towards the path of freedom
as it fills your souls with sustenance.
Let reason take hold of your spirit
and allow it to draw you towards the light of truth and justice.

Let the innocence of children be a model
for they do not judge another based on race or faith.
Let the child, who has not been tainted by man's awful ways, lead the way of mankind
for the rest of us close our eyes in the day, only to open them at night.
Beauty lies only in the heart of a person
so clear your conscience if you judged a man on something else.

Let love unite one another
and let the affection flow freely through your veins.
Treat each man as your father
and each woman as your mother.

The Jewish man and woman is like the Christian man and woman
and the Christian man and woman is like the Muslim man and woman.

Let these arrows of truth pierce your heart
and unshackle the dark chains that have taken hold of your innocence.
We come from the same tree of life
yet in the form of different fruits.
We are all brothers and sisters
separated at birth and put on different paths.
At the end of our journey we will be reunited under the rays of the sun
and will gaze in awe and wonder as we stare into the aged faces of our kin.
Make haste and hold one another
and never let evil thoughts of inequality seize your minds again.

Never succumb to the will of those who seek to destroy your way of life
for the truth of life streams from within yourself.
Go and purify your souls in the water of wisdom,
let it make your heart light, your soul pure, and your mind free.
Let freedom rule these lands
and the traditions of your ancestors flourish like the crops of the Nile.

Go and sit under the shade of the tree of wisdom and prepare for a life of reason
and do not forbid yourself what your soul desires.
Let the white doves dance in the cloudless sky
and the earth take its natural course around the sun."

Footnotes Appendices

[I] Graham, Dave. "New book reveals horror of Nazi camp brothels." *Reuters*. N.p., 17 Aug. 2009. Web. 3 May 2016.

[II] Radhika, Sanghani. "The horrific story of Korea's 'comfort women' - forced to be sex slaves during World War Two." *The Telegraph*. N.p., 29 Dec. 2015. Web. 3 May 2016.

[III] Hartenstein, Meena. "Beck claims 10% of Muslims are terrorists; Zakaria blasts him for fuzzy math." *NY Daily News*. N.p., 13 Dec. 2010. Web. 6 Apr. 2016.

[IV] Kurzman, Charles. "Muslim-American Involvement with Violent Extremism, 2016." *Triangle Center on Terrorism and Homeland Security*. Duke University, 26 Jan. 2017. Web. 15 Mar. 2017.

[V] Federal Bureau of Investigation. "Terrorism 2002-2005." *FBI*. U.S. Department of Justice, n.d. Web. 21 Apr. 2015.

[VI] "Celebrating the birth of Christ while preserving our Islamic identity." *Baynnat*. Trans. Ghassan. N.p., 16 Dec. 2014. Web. 6 Feb. 2016.

[VII] "A Conversation with Sahar Amer, Author of 'What is Veiling?'." A Conversation with Sahar Amer, Author of 'What is Veiling?'. Duke Islamic Studies Center, 22 Sept. 2014. Web. 17 May 2017.

[VIII] Aghajanian, Liana. "The Complicated History of Headscarves." *Racked*. Ed. Julia Rubin. N.p., 20 Dec. 2016. Web. 5 Mar. 2017.

[IX] Richman, Cynthia. "Gender and Legal History Paper Summary." *Georgetown Law*. Georgetown Law Library, n.d. Web. 19 June 2017.

[X] Taylor, Humphrey. "While Most Americans Believe in God, Only 36% Attend a Religious Service Once a Month or More Often." *The Harris Poll*. Harris Interactive, 15 Oct. 2003. Web. 2 Apr. 2016.

[XI] "111832: Ruling on a Muslim entering a church." *Islam Question and Answer*. N.p., 4 Jan. 2012. Web. 2 Sept. 2015. <https://islamqa.info>.

Endnotes

[i] Gerson, Michael. "Herman Cain's modern-day religious test." *The Washington Post*. N.p., 20 June 2011. Web. 27 July 2013.
[ii] "McCaffrey, Shannon. "Gingrich sets a demand for Muslim office-seekers." *Yahoo News*. N.p., 17 Jan. 2012. Web. 14 Dec. 2015.
[iii] Bershad, Jon. "Glenn Beck Guesses 10% Of Muslims Are Terrorists (UPDATE)." *Mediaite*. N.p., 6 Dec. 2010. Web. 8 Feb. 2015
[iv] LaCasse, Alexander. "How many Muslim extremists are there? Just the facts, please." *The Christian Science Monitor*. N.p., 13 Jan. 2015. Web. 7 Apr. 2015.
[v] Katrandjian, Olivia. "Iraqi Woman Beaten to Death in California, Hate Crime Suspected." *ABC News*. N.p., 25 Mar. 2012. Web. 30 Apr. 2015.
[vi] ""Video Shows Fla. Shooting of Man Asked About Being Muslim." *CAIR*. N.p., 4 Jan. 2013. Web. 9 Feb. 2015.
[vii] "Schenk, Mary. "Bond at $500,000 in attack on UI professor." *The News Gazette*. N.p., 8 Dec. 2011. Web. 17 Dec. 2015.
[viii] Jimenez, Eddie. "California mosque vandalized, Ground Zero mentioned." *McClatchy DC Bureau*. N.p., 25 Aug. 2010. Web. 27 May 2015.
[ix] Marcum, Diana. "Vandalism at Madera mosque one of several incidents under investigation by Justice Department." *LA Times*. N.p., 7 Sept. 2010. Web. 6 Dec. 2015.
[x] "Texas panel votes to limit references to Islam." *Boston*. Globe Newspaper Company, 25 Sept. 2010. Web. 2 June 2015.
[xi] "Hauss, Kimberlee. "Muslim Woman Denied Foster Care Because Of No-Pork Rule." *Huffington Post*. N.p., 15 June 2010. Web. 17 July 2015.
[xii] Culp-Ressler, Tara. "Louisiana Republican Supports State Funds For Religious Schools, As Long As They're Not Islamic." *ThinkProgress*. N.p., 6 July 2012. Web. 9 July 2015.
[xiii] "Stein, Sam. "Gabriela Mercer, Arizona GOP Candidate: Middle Eastern Immigrants Want 'To Harm' The U.S." *Huffington P*ost. N.p., 28 Aug. 2012. Web. 8 July 2015.
[xiv] Wing, Nick. "Republicans Have Strongly Negative Views Of Muslims, Arabs: Poll." *Huffington P*ost. N.p., 23 Aug. 2012. Web. 8 July 2015.
[xv] Matthew 5:17, *New International Version*. Biblica, n.d. Web. 4 Mar. 2016. <Biblegateway.com>.
[xvi] An-Nahl 16:106, *Towards Understanding The Quran*. Trans. Zafar Ishaq Ansari. Leicester: The Islamic Foundation, 1988. Print.
[xvii] *Al Tabiri*: Tafsir, Bulak 1323 sqq.24.122
[xviii] Ghafir 40:28, *Towards Understanding The Quran*. Trans. Zafar Ishaq Ansari.

Leicester: The Islamic Foundation, 1988. Print.
^{xix} An-Nisa 4:34, *Towards Understanding The Quran*. Trans. Zafar Ishaq Ansari. Leicester: The Islamic Foundation, 1988. Print.
^{xx} An-Nisa 4:94, *Towards Understanding The Quran*. Trans. Zafar Ishaq Ansari. Leicester: The Islamic Foundation, 1988. Print.
^{xxi} Abu Dawud: Book 11, Number 2139
^{xxii} Muslim: Book 1, Number 142
^{xxiii} Al-Waqiah 56: 75-80, *Towards Understanding The Quran*. Trans. Zafar Ishaq Ansari. Leicester: The Islamic Foundation, 1988. Print.
^{xxiv} An-Nisa 4:124, *Towards Understanding The Quran*. Trans. Zafar Ishaq Ansari. Leicester: The Islamic Foundation, 1988. Print.
^{xxv} An-Nahl 16:97, *Towards Understanding The Quran*. Trans. Zafar Ishaq Ansari. Leicester: The Islamic Foundation, 1988. Print
^{xxvi} Ghafir 40:40, *Towards Understanding The Quran*. Trans. Zafar Ishaq Ansari. Leicester: The Islamic Foundation, 1988. Print.
^{xxvii} Al-Imran 3:195, *Towards Understanding The Quran*. Trans. Zafar Ishaq Ansari. Leicester: The Islamic Foundation, 1988. Print.
^{xxviii} Al- Baqarah 2:282, *Towards Understanding The Quran*. Trans. Zafar Ishaq Ansari. Leicester: The Islamic Foundation, 1988. Print.
^{xxix} An-Nur 24:6-9, *Towards Understanding The Quran*. Trans. Zafar Ishaq Ansari. Leicester: The Islamic Foundation, 1988. Print.
^{xxx} An-Nisa 4:11-12, *Towards Understanding The Quran*. Trans. Zafar Ishaq Ansari. Leicester: The Islamic Foundation, 1988. Print.
^{xxxi} Al-Muminun 23:1-6, *Towards Understanding The Quran*. Trans. Zafar Ishaq Ansari. Leicester: The Islamic Foundation, 1988. Print.
^{xxxii} An-Nur 24:33, *Towards Understanding The Quran*. Trans. Zafar Ishaq Ansari. Leicester: The Islamic Foundation, 1988. Print.
^{xxxiii} An-Nur 24:32, *Towards Understanding The Quran*. Trans. Zafar Ishaq Ansari. Leicester: The Islamic Foundation, 1988. Print.
^{xxxiv} Bukhari: Volume 1, Book 3, Number 97
^{xxxv} Muslim: Book 15, Number 4078
^{xxxvi} Al-Shafi'i, Kitabul Umm. Vol.3, p.253.
^{xxxvii} Bukhari: Volume 8, Book 73, Number 2
^{xxxviii} Al-Araf 7:20, *Towards Understanding The Quran*. Trans. Zafar Ishaq Ansari. Leicester: The Islamic Foundation, 1988. Print.
^{xxxix} Al-Araf 7:23, *Towards Understanding The Quran*. Trans. Zafar Ishaq Ansari. Leicester: The Islamic Foundation, 1988. Print.
^{xl} Al-Ahzab 33:35, *Towards Understanding The Quran*. Trans. Zafar Ishaq Ansari. Leicester: The Islamic Foundation, 1988. Print.
^{xli} An-Nisa 4:124, *Towards Understanding The Quran*. Trans. Zafar Ishaq Ansari. Leicester: The Islamic Foundation, 1988. Print.
^{xlii} Bukhari: Volume 7, Book 62, Number 1
^{xliii} Bukhari: Volume 7, Book 62, Number 88
^{xliv} Bukhari: Volume 4, Book 52, Number 41.
^{xlv} At-Talaq 65:4, *Towards Understanding The Quran*. Trans. Zafar Ishaq Ansari.

Leicester: The Islamic Foundation, 1988. Print.

[xlvi] Ar-Rum 30:21, *Towards Understanding The Quran*. Trans. Zafar Ishaq Ansari. Leicester: The Islamic Foundation, 1988. Print.

[xlvii] An-Nisa 4:19, *Towards Understanding The Quran*. Trans. Zafar Ishaq Ansari. Leicester: The Islamic Foundation, 1988. Print.

[xlviii] At-Taubah 9:5, *Towards Understanding The Quran*. Trans. Zafar Ishaq Ansari. Leicester: The Islamic Foundation, 1988. Print.

[xlix] Al-Fajr 89:17-20, *Towards Understanding The Quran*. Trans. Zafar Ishaq Ansari. Leicester: The Islamic Foundation, 1988. Print.

[l] Attributed to Ja`far ibn Abī Tālib, elder brother of Imam Ali, and cousin to the Prophet Muhammad

[li] Ibn Hisham: 1/334-338

[lii] At-Taubah 9:1-4, *Towards Understanding The Quran*. Trans. Zafar Ishaq Ansari. Leicester: The Islamic Foundation, 1988. Print.

[liii] At-Taubah 9:5, *Towards Understanding The Quran*. Trans. Zafar Ishaq Ansari. Leicester: The Islamic Foundation, 1988. Print.

[liv] At-Taubah 9:6, *Towards Understanding The Quran*. Trans. Zafar Ishaq Ansari. Leicester: The Islamic Foundation, 1988. Print.

[lv] Al-Baqarah 2:191, *Towards Understanding The Quran*. Trans. Zafar Ishaq Ansari. Leicester: The Islamic Foundation, 1988. Print.

[lvi] Al-Baqarah 2:190, *Towards Understanding The Quran*. Trans. Zafar Ishaq Ansari. Leicester: The Islamic Foundation, 1988. Print.

[lvii] Al-Baqarah 2:192, *Towards Understanding The Quran*. Trans. Zafar Ishaq Ansari. Leicester: The Islamic Foundation, 1988. Print.

[lviii] Al-Baqarah 2:194, *Towards Understanding The Quran*. Trans. Zafar Ishaq Ansari. Leicester: The Islamic Foundation, 1988. Print.

[lix] Al-Ma'idah 5:32, *Towards Understanding The Quran*. Trans. Zafar Ishaq Ansari. Leicester: The Islamic Foundation, 1988. Print.

[lx] Muslim: Book 19, Number 4418

[lxi] Ya Sin 36:18, *Towards Understanding The Quran*. Trans. Zafar Ishaq Ansari. Leicester: The Islamic Foundation, 1988. Print.

[lxii] Al-Baqarah 2:256, *Towards Understanding The Quran*. Trans. Zafar Ishaq Ansari. Leicester: The Islamic Foundation, 1988. Print.

[lxiii] Al-Kahf 18:29, *Towards Understanding The Quran*. Trans. Zafar Ishaq Ansari. Leicester: The Islamic Foundation, 1988. Print.

[lxiv] Yunnus 10:99, *Towards Understanding The Quran*. Trans. Zafar Ishaq Ansari. Leicester: The Islamic Foundation, 1988. Print.

[lxv] An-Nur 24:2, *Towards Understanding The Quran*. Trans. Zafar Ishaq Ansari. Leicester: The Islamic Foundation, 1988. Print.

[lxvi] An-Nisa 4:25, *Towards Understanding The Quran*. Trans. Zafar Ishaq Ansari. Leicester: The Islamic Foundation, 1988. Print.

[lxvii] John 8:7. *New International Version*. Biblica, n.d. Web. 4 Mar. 2016. <Biblegateway.com>.

[lxviii] An-Nur 24:4-5, *Towards Understanding The Quran*. Trans. Zafar Ishaq Ansari. Leicester: The Islamic Foundation, 1988. Print.

[lxix] Al-Furqan 25:70, *Towards Understanding The Quran.* Trans. Zafar Ishaq Ansari. Leicester: The Islamic Foundation, 1988. Print.
[lxx] Al-Tirmidhi: Volume 4, Book 12, Number 2562
[lxxi] Ad-Dukhan 44:51-55, *Towards Understanding The Quran.* Trans. Zafar Ishaq Ansari. Leicester: The Islamic Foundation, 1988. Print.
[lxxii] At-Tur 52:20, *Towards Understanding The Quran.* Trans. Zafar Ishaq Ansari. Leicester: The Islamic Foundation, 1988. Print.
[lxxiii] Ar-Rad 13:23-24, *Towards Understanding The Quran.* Trans. Zafar Ishaq Ansari. Leicester: The Islamic Foundation, 1988. Print.
[lxxiv] Al-Hajj 22:23, *Towards Understanding The Quran.* Trans. Zafar Ishaq Ansari. Leicester: The Islamic Foundation, 1988. Print.
[lxxv] Al-Haqqah 69:21, *Towards Understanding The Quran.* Trans. Zafar Ishaq Ansari. Leicester: The Islamic Foundation, 1988. Print.
[lxxvi] Al-Waqiah 56:10-12, *Towards Understanding The Quran.* Trans. Zafar Ishaq Ansari. Leicester: The Islamic Foundation, 1988. Print.
[lxxvii] Az-Zukhruf 43:70, *Towards Understanding The Quran.* Trans. Zafar Ishaq Ansari. Leicester: The Islamic Foundation, 1988. Print.
[lxxviii] At-Taubah 9:72, *Towards Understanding The Quran.* Trans. Zafar Ishaq Ansari. Leicester: The Islamic Foundation, 1988. Print.
[lxxix] Exodus 21:20-21. *New International Version.* Biblica, n.d. Web. 4 Mar. 2016. <Biblegateway.com>.
[lxxx] Deuteronomy 20:10-14 5:17. *New International Version.* Biblica, n.d. Web. 4 Mar. 2016. <Biblegateway.com>.
[lxxxi] An-Nisa 4:48, *Towards Understanding The Quran.* Trans. Zafar Ishaq Ansari. Leicester: The Islamic Foundation, 1988. Print.
[lxxxii] Az-Zumar 39:65, *Towards Understanding The Quran.* Trans. Zafar Ishaq Ansari. Leicester: The Islamic Foundation, 1988. Print.
[lxxxiii] Al-Baqarah 2:177, *Towards Understanding The Quran.* Trans. Zafar Ishaq Ansari. Leicester: The Islamic Foundation, 1988. Print.
[lxxxiv] At-Taubah 9:60, *Towards Understanding The Quran.* Trans. Zafar Ishaq Ansari. Leicester: The Islamic Foundation, 1988. Print.
[lxxxv] Muslim: Book 15, Number 4088
[lxxxvi] Muslim: Book 15, Number 4078
[lxxxvii] Abu Dawud: Book 41, Number 4957
[lxxxviii] Luqman 31:6, *Towards Understanding The Quran.* Trans. Zafar Ishaq Ansari. Leicester: The Islamic Foundation, 1988. Print.
[lxxxix] Bukhari: Volume 7, Book 69, Number 494
[xc] Bukhari: Volume 4, Book 56, Number 730
[xci] Bukhari: Volume 2, Book 6, Number 1090
[xcii] Tirmidhi: Book 49, Number 4054
[xciii] Bihar al-Anwar: Volume 79, Number 2
[xciv] Al-Anbiya 21:107, *Towards Understanding The Quran.* Trans. Zafar Ishaq Ansari. Leicester: The Islamic Foundation, 1988. Print.
[xcv] An-Nahl 16:58-59, *Towards Understanding The Quran.* Trans. Zafar Ishaq Ansari. Leicester: The Islamic Foundation, 1988. Print.

[xcvi] At-Tawkir 81:8-9, *Towards Understanding The Quran*. Trans. Zafar Ishaq Ansari. Leicester: The Islamic Foundation, 1988. Print.
[xcvii] An-Nisa 4:4, *Towards Understanding The Quran*. Trans. Zafar Ishaq Ansari. Leicester: The Islamic Foundation, 1988. Print.
[xcviii] Ar-Rum 30:13, *Towards Understanding The Quran*. Trans. Zafar Ishaq Ansari. Leicester: The Islamic Foundation, 1988. Print.
[xcix] Al-Maidah 5:48, *Towards Understanding The Quran*. Trans. Zafar Ishaq Ansari. Leicester: The Islamic Foundation, 1988. Print.
[c] Bukhari: Book 18, Number 1645
[ci] Ar-Rum 30:30, *Towards Understanding The Quran*. Trans. Zafar Ishaq Ansari. Leicester: The Islamic Foundation, 1988. Print.
[cii] Ta Ha 20:94, *Towards Understanding The Quran*. Trans. Zafar Ishaq Ansari. Leicester: The Islamic Foundation, 1988. Print.
[ciii] Bukhari: Volume 7, Book 72, Number 780
[civ] Bukhari: Volume 4, Book 55, Number 668
[cv] An-Nisa 4:116-119, *Towards Understanding The Quran*. Trans. Zafar Ishaq Ansari. Leicester: The Islamic Foundation, 1988. Print.
[cvi] Tirmidhi: Volume 5, Book 39, Number 2678
[cvii] Tirmidhi: Volume 5, Book 41, Hadith 2763
[cviii] 1 Corinthains 11:4-16 8: 7. *New International Version*. Biblica, n.d. Web. 4 Mar. 2016. <Biblegateway.com>.
[cix] An-Nur 24:31, *Towards Understanding The Quran*. Trans. Zafar Ishaq Ansari. Leicester: The Islamic Foundation, 1988. Print.
[cx] Al-Araf 7:46, *Towards Understanding The Quran*. Trans. Zafar Ishaq Ansari. Leicester: The Islamic Foundation, 1988. Print.
[cxi] Maryam 19:16-17, *Towards Understanding The Quran*. Trans. Zafar Ishaq Ansari. Leicester: The Islamic Foundation, 1988. Print.
[cxii] Al-Ahzab 33:53, *Towards Understanding The Quran*. Trans. Zafar Ishaq Ansari. Leicester: The Islamic Foundation, 1988. Print.
[cxiii] Fussilat 41:5, *Towards Understanding The Quran*. Trans. Zafar Ishaq Ansari. Leicester: The Islamic Foundation, 1988. Print.
[cxiv] Ash-Shura 42:51, *Towards Understanding The Quran*. Trans. Zafar Ishaq Ansari. Leicester: The Islamic Foundation, 1988. Print.
[cxv] Al-Ahzab 33:59, *Towards Understanding The Quran*. Trans. Zafar Ishaq Ansari. Leicester: The Islamic Foundation, 1988. Print.
[cxvi] An-Nur 24:30, *Towards Understanding The Quran*. Trans. Zafar Ishaq Ansari. Leicester: The Islamic Foundation, 1988. Print.
[cxvii] An-Nur 24:31, *Towards Understanding The Quran*. Trans. Zafar Ishaq Ansari. Leicester: The Islamic Foundation, 1988. Print.
[cxviii] Al-Baqarah 2:221, *Towards Understanding The Quran*. Trans. Zafar Ishaq Ansari. Leicester: The Islamic Foundation, 1988. Print.
[cxix] Al-Maidah 5:5, *Towards Understanding The Quran*. Trans. Zafar Ishaq Ansari. Leicester: The Islamic Foundation, 1988. Print.
[cxx] Al-Baqarah 2:35-37, *Towards Understanding The Quran*. Trans. Zafar Ishaq Ansari. Leicester: The Islamic Foundation, 1988. Print.

cxxi Ash-Shuara 26:14, *Towards Understanding The Quran*. Trans. Zafar Ishaq Ansari. Leicester: The Islamic Foundation, 1988. Print.
cxxii Hud 11:45-47, *Towards Understanding The Quran*. Trans. Zafar Ishaq Ansari. Leicester: The Islamic Foundation, 1988. Print.
cxxiii At-Taubah 9:113, *Towards Understanding The Quran*. Trans. Zafar Ishaq Ansari. Leicester: The Islamic Foundation, 1988. Print.
cxxiv Sad 38:79-83, *Towards Understanding The Quran*. Trans. Zafar Ishaq Ansari. Leicester: The Islamic Foundation, 1988. Print.
cxxv Al-Imran 3:45, *Towards Understanding The Quran*. Trans. Zafar Ishaq Ansari. Leicester: The Islamic Foundation, 1988. Print.
cxxvi Maryam 19:19-21, *Towards Understanding The Quran*. Trans. Zafar Ishaq Ansari. Leicester: The Islamic Foundation, 1988. Print.
cxxvii Al-Anbiya 21:91, *Towards Understanding The Quran*. Trans. Zafar Ishaq Ansari. Leicester: The Islamic Foundation, 1988. Print.
cxxviii Al-Imran 3:49, *Towards Understanding The Quran*. Trans. Zafar Ishaq Ansari. Leicester: The Islamic Foundation, 1988. Print.
cxxix Al-Maidah 5:46, *Towards Understanding The Quran*. Trans. Zafar Ishaq Ansari. Leicester: The Islamic Foundation, 1988. Print.
cxxx Al-Hadid 57:27, *Towards Understanding The Quran*. Trans. Zafar Ishaq Ansari. Leicester: The Islamic Foundation, 1988. Print.
cxxxi Al-Imran 3:55, *Towards Understanding The Quran*. Trans. Zafar Ishaq Ansari. Leicester: The Islamic Foundation, 1988. Print.
cxxxii An-Nisa 4:171, *Towards Understanding The Quran*. Trans. Zafar Ishaq Ansari. Leicester: The Islamic Foundation, 1988. Print.
cxxxiii Al-Maidah 5:116, *Towards Understanding The Quran*. Trans. Zafar Ishaq Ansari. Leicester: The Islamic Foundation, 1988. Print.
cxxxiv Al-Maidah 5:75, *Towards Understanding The Quran*. Trans. Zafar Ishaq Ansari. Leicester: The Islamic Foundation, 1988. Print.
cxxxv Maryam 19:30-31, *Towards Understanding The Quran*. Trans. Zafar Ishaq Ansari. Leicester: The Islamic Foundation, 1988. Print.
cxxxvi Al-Imran 3:54, *Towards Understanding The Quran*. Trans. Zafar Ishaq Ansari. Leicester: The Islamic Foundation, 1988. Print.
cxxxvii An-Nisa 4:157-158, *Towards Understanding The Quran*. Trans. Zafar Ishaq Ansari. Leicester: The Islamic Foundation, 1988. Print.
cxxxviii Al-Baqarah 2:37, *Towards Understanding The Quran*. Trans. Zafar Ishaq Ansari. Leicester: The Islamic Foundation, 1988. Print.
cxxxix Al-Anam 6:164, *Towards Understanding The Quran*. Trans. Zafar Ishaq Ansari. Leicester: The Islamic Foundation, 1988. Print.
cxl Al-Hajj 22:37, *Towards Understanding The Quran*. Trans. Zafar Ishaq Ansari. Leicester: The Islamic Foundation, 1988. Print.
cxli Az-Zumar 39:53, *Towards Understanding The Quran*. Trans. Zafar Ishaq Ansari. Leicester: The Islamic Foundation, 1988. Print.
cxlii Al-Baqarah 2:183, *Towards Understanding The Quran*. Trans. Zafar Ishaq Ansari. Leicester: The Islamic Foundation, 1988. Print.
cxliii Al-Baqarah 2:184, *Towards Understanding The Quran*. Trans. Zafar Ishaq

Ansari. Leicester: The Islamic Foundation, 1988. Print.

[cxliv] Az-Zumar 39:46, *Towards Understanding The Quran*. Trans. Zafar Ishaq Ansari. Leicester: The Islamic Foundation, 1988. Print.

[cxlv] Al-Maidah 5:69, *Towards Understanding The Quran*. Trans. Zafar Ishaq Ansari. Leicester: The Islamic Foundation, 1988. Print.

[cxlvi] Al-Maidah 5:69 Towards Understanding the Quran, UK: Islamic Foundation. Islamicstudies.info. Web. 9 Mar. 2013.

[cxlvii] Al-Isra 17:15, *Towards Understanding The Quran*. Trans. Zafar Ishaq Ansari. Leicester: The Islamic Foundation, 1988. Print.

[cxlviii] Al-Imran 3:85, *Towards Understanding The Quran*. Trans. Zafar Ishaq Ansari. Leicester: The Islamic Foundation, 1988. Print.

[cxlix] Ad-Dhariyat 51:56, *Towards Understanding The Quran*. Trans. Zafar Ishaq Ansari. Leicester: The Islamic Foundation, 1988. Print.

[cl] Al-Baqarah 2:21, *Towards Understanding The Quran*. Trans. Zafar Ishaq Ansari. Leicester: The Islamic Foundation, 1988. Print.

[cli] Al-Ankabut 29:45, *Towards Understanding The Quran*. Trans. Zafar Ishaq Ansari. Leicester: The Islamic Foundation, 1988. Print.

[clii] Al-Imran 3:67, *Towards Understanding The Quran*. Trans. Zafar Ishaq Ansari. Leicester: The Islamic Foundation, 1988. Print.

[cliii] Yunus 10:84, *Towards Understanding The Quran*. Trans. Zafar Ishaq Ansari. Leicester: The Islamic Foundation, 1988. Print.

[cliv] Ash-Shura 42:13, *Towards Understanding The Quran*. Trans. Zafar Ishaq Ansari. Leicester: The Islamic Foundation, 1988. Print.

[clv] Al-Muminum 23:52-53, *Towards Understanding The Quran*. Trans. Zafar Ishaq Ansari. Leicester: The Islamic Foundation, 1988. Print.

[clvi] Al-Imran 3:103, *Towards Understanding The Quran*. Trans. Zafar Ishaq Ansari. Leicester: The Islamic Foundation, 1988. Print.

www.ingramcontent.com/pod-product-compliance
Lightning Source LLC
Chambersburg PA
CBHW061324040426
42444CB00011B/2772